the EMPOWERED Woman

ALSO BY J. NICOLE WILLIAMSON

Being Fathered for a Divine Purpose
Heaven's Secret of Success
The Esther Mandate
Freedom in the Light

AVAILABLE FROM KING'S LANTERN PUBLISHING

the EMPOWERED Woman

RESTORING WOMEN TO THEIR TRUE IDENTITY

J. NICOLE WILLIAMSON

King's Lantern Publishing

The Empowered Woman

Copyright © 2014 J. Nicole Williamson

Revised Edition

King's Lantern Publishing
www.kingslantern.com
Allen, TX 75013

Printed in the United States of America

Library of Congress Control Number: 2014902189

ISBN-10 0985139641

ISBN-13 978-0-9851396-4-3

Quotes used with permission.

Unless otherwise indicated, Scripture quotations are taken from the New American Standard Bible ®, Copyright © 1960, 1962, 1963, 1968, 1971, 1972, 1973, 1975, 1977, 1995 by the Lockman Foundation. Used with permission. (www.Lockman.org)

Cover Design: Kristin Joya

To my daughter, Bethany, I pray that you will walk in the celebration, dignity, courage, and freedom of your identity as a woman created in God's image. The world is waiting for His likeness to be manifest through you.

To my son, Daniel, that you might know your own true identity as a man created in the image of God, and for the work He has for you to do together with the men and women who will come alongside you.

Acknowledgments

My wonderful husband, Ken—you have truly been for me a man of God's likeness and love. Thank you for being a godly husband and father whose love has launched our family into a fruitful destiny. Thank you for believing in me and for releasing the gifts of God within me for His purposes.

My mother—I am grateful for the years that we journeyed together before your going home. Your influence and prayers are the stepping-stones of who I am today.

ENDORSEMENTS

Every woman on the planet needs to read this book! The work of the serpent in Eden to deceive and strip the first couple of their true identity and God's purpose for them is artfully exposed in Nicole's book, *The Empowered Woman*. Cultural mindsets fueled by the father of lies will be broken. You will be freed, restored, and healed to rise up to pursue the destiny and calling your heavenly Father designed for you out of His eternal wisdom and heart of love! Nicole beautifully reveals Creator God's work in fashioning His image, likeness and nature into Eden's first couple, as well as uncovering the picture of the Last Adam's Bride, the glorious church — genderless and without spot or wrinkle! It will bring you to tears! Well done, Nicole! Your journey is an inspiration for all women, and men too!

—**Jean Hodges**
Federation of Ministers & Churches International

Identity crisis! Inner conflict! Warfare! These are only a few of the challenges facing women today that hold many captive. Nicole's book, *The Empowered Woman*, brings freedom through powerful biblical and historical interpretation. Nicole's own personal journey helps readers to understand the path to freedom that is available to them. She also paints a beautiful picture of the way God created man and woman to live together and bring glory to the Lord. I highly recommend this book to both men and women. Implementing the principles in *The Empowered Woman* will help women arise and fulfill God's destiny for their lives!

—**Barbara Wentroble**
President, International Breakthrough Ministries
President, Business Owners for Christ International

The goal of ministry is to mature men and women to their destiny. Nicole details the impact and practical value of women, not just in ministry, but in value. This is another great work by J. Nicole Williamson that may just change the way you think about women, and the real value of the daughters of God. Having championed the call of women in ministry, I would love to have had this book years ago. I encourage you to read *The Empowered Woman*.

— **Dr. Randy Speed**
Sr. Leader, River of Glory
Plano, TX

Exciting! Enlightening! Energizing! *The Empowered Woman* is a must read for every woman who has struggled to understand who she is. Nicole has written an easy to read, historically accurate, and biblically based explanation of the enemy's plot against women since the beginning of time. Every woman who begins reading this book will find they cannot put it down! Women will receive healing and freedom from the bondage of wrong thinking (theirs and others) as they read. Nicole shows that women have a voice…in their home, their ministries, and in the Body of Christ at large. It is His voice! She clarifies our call to step up and step out into our God-given destiny! I will recommend *The Empowered Woman* to all of my friends…both men and women. It really has been written "for such a time as this!"

— **Rev. Dr. MaryAnn Robertson**
Founder, High Place Ministries
Founder, Women of the Kingdom

Knowing your identity can transform your life! Nicole's book, *The Empowered Woman*, is encouraging, enlightening, informative, biblical and historically based. It will lift the hearts and change the mindsets of anyone reading it, male or female. Nicole has gone to great lengths to establish the truths of God's Word regarding women and the issues they have faced through the ages, and many still face today. God created man (male and female) in His own image—why would one have less value? Satan even posed the question of identity to Jesus, "If you are the Son of God..." to which Jesus answered, "It is written." I highly recommend this book to men and women, as it expresses in such a powerful, gracious way the original intent of God for men and women—to walk together and fulfill His purposes in the earth as His Body, with equal respect and value.

—Carol Torrance
U.S. Director, Aglow International

Some who feel it is more for a man to say these things regarding a "woman's place" is the reason this book had to be written and is a must read for men and women alike. So, let me be the man who says it: I give you permission to read this book as if I, as a man, had written it, and then give the credit to its true author, a woman! This book will set hearers free, especially those denominationalists that still believe the cross only broke the curse off of men, and women just have to endure until the end. Nicole's insights on our identity as Sons and the Bride of the Last Adam are power and mind renewing. Women, read *The Empowered Woman*! Arise and be encouraged to fulfill your destiny. Men, step into your rightful place and release women from the bondage to tradition to walk in her biblical and spiritual call. Yes, Nicole, it is about time!

—Randy Hill
Senior Leader, Summit Church, Wylie, TX
President, Encounter Ministries International
Author, *Encounters: Stories of Healing*

The Empowered Woman provides a critical missing truth to the Christian Church. It is well researched and the male-female relationship is scripturally addressed with clarity and historical cultural contexts. This book is a transforming message of great encouragement!

—Marie Perusek, MD
VP Central TX, Aglow International

Wow is all I can say about *The Empowered Woman*! Women need to read this book—it is so freeing. I was enlightened by it. I too was that woman in bondage when the Lord told me I was going to preach and I said, "But I am a woman!" And He said, "I know that!" Thanks, Nicole for hearing and sharing our Father's heart for women who are bound in tradition, to see them flourish and do what God has called them to do, just as I am doing as a Native American woman. We have a voice, "Let My daughters go!"

— **Apostle Sue Chancellor**
Pastor, Holy Mtn. Praise & Worship Center
Kenwood, Oklahoma

Nicole is a first rate writer. She handles her topic, a controversial one, with great finesse and femininity. Her topic of restoring women to their true identity is well researched both biblically and historically. She brings revelation and clarification on the woman's role in God's divine creative plan that will set women free. *The Empowered Woman* is a must read and hard to put down. This is your "go to" book on finding your identity in Christ and in the Body.

— **Jenny Juhl**
Minister, Assistant Director CFN/FMC
Presbyter, Christ for the Nations/
Fellowship of Ministers & Churches

The Empowered Woman is a must read for every woman and man! It is filled with thought provoking and life-changing truths. Biblical perspectives bring balanced understanding and clarity to the grey areas that most have struggled with their whole life because of environments that shaped us.

— **Alisa Burns**
Author, *Loving Beyond Limits*

Table of Contents

FOREWORD

The 21st century church is in major transition as her landscape is undergoing definite change. Apostle Jim Hodges sees the major changes in the church today as primarily structural, referring to the New Apostolic Reformation wineskin that goes beyond superficial alterations of style and presentation. He is speaking of major reform that is realigning the church with that of God's original design and pattern of *Genesis 1:28*. While some find this a painful time, most Kingdom-minded leaders are embracing it as our finest hour. Nicole Williamson is one such leader. She has a deep passion for the Kingdom of God and a burden to see the women of God empowered and released to fulfill their truth-liberated purpose and destiny in Christ.

This book is an excellent biblical study of God's original design of the male and female as they relate to the church and the culture. Both are to be strong, carry the passion fire for the kingdom of God, and rule the earth in Christ. This occurs when each is in union and harmony with the other, and yet each is also able to freely operate in the unique gifting, calling, and anointing given them by the Father. The uniqueness and union of the two generate an exponential synergy of authority and power needed to fulfill God's original intent for the male, the female, the church, and the culture.

The misinterpretations of the role of women in the home and the church have done much, throughout history, to impede the female from stepping into her full calling in God. Nicole does an excellent job of clarifying these misrepresentations by the traditional church. She brings to light the life of scripture as she paves the way of truth that women are not second-class citizens in the Kingdom of God. Women and men are both "spiritual Adam" with unique gifts for ministry that are of God's choosing, and the critical role of the woman in equipping the saints for the work of ministry is no less important than that of the man.

We have been fortunate throughout our years of training and ministry to be untainted by gender bias regarding ministers of the gospel. Our experience is that we are ALL able ministers of the gospel through our faith in Christ. As Paul says, *"There is neither Jew nor Greek, slave nor free, male nor female, for you are all one in Christ Jesus" (Galatians 3: 28).* Women throughout scripture have always had a prominent role in expanding the kingdom of God in their time. To paraphrase the author, scripture validates that women are to be actively engaged in praying, speaking, teaching, and leading as builders of the church and the culture. Clearly, each minister of the gospel, male and female alike, is critical in expressing the fullness of Christ and in completing God's original kingdom purpose in the earth before His return.

This book addresses a very real and heavy topic. Nicole navigates it much like a surgeon who makes precision cuts to perform a delicate operation. She is a skilled writer, a knowledgeable teacher of the word, and a woman of excellence. Take her hand and let her walk you through the pages of this book. She will guide you through the minefield of religious tradition and bring you through into truth and freedom.

— Pastors Larry and Kathy Burden
Kingdom Life International
Frisco, Texas

INTRODUCTION

They say that the area of your struggle often becomes the platform of your message. Martin Luther King, a pastor from Alabama, rose up in the 1960's with his message "I have a dream." His dream was to see people of all races receive justice and an equal place in U.S. society—one that had been denied many for a long time.

I, too, have a dream—to see the world celebrate the full worth and value of women, and to see women walk in freedom to fulfill the destiny that God has for them. Through the centuries, women have often been suppressed in culture and religion simply because of their gender. But God wants to change that. He wants His daughters fully present and flourishing in this hour. Why? Because we, together with godly men, reflect the image of God on earth. And God wants to be known.

In 2010, my mother passed away into eternity. Months before she crossed into glory, she shared with me her disappointment in feeling that she hadn't fully lived her destiny on earth. The reason sprang from a sense of not being affirmed or fully released into her gifts and calling in God.

As a Christian woman, she waited for my father to be the "proper head and priest of the home" who would lift her into her full potential. But because he didn't, she felt she couldn't. Even when opportunities and invitations to ministry were extended to her, she declined because she *knew* that dad would say "no."

Whether such prohibitions were real or perceived or both, I've learned that destiny isn't so much what another person believes about us, as much as what we believe about ourselves. What are the permissions or limitations that we impose upon our

17

own life? For many years, I embraced many personal prohibitions and limitations regarding my calling in God, because I believed the limiting messages in culture and religion regarding my female gender. Then God took me on a journey of identity in Him—where the Father gives me full permission, as His daughter, to thrive freely in divine destiny.

It takes both men and women to not only produce the generations that form the world's nations, but it takes both to heal and parent them. Only as we understand the value of both male and female in God's image can we fulfill God's plan for us, *and* for the world in which we live.

To grasp this valuable knowledge, we must go back to the beginning, back to the garden and see God's original design…one that was lost at the Fall but restored in Christ. Only when we see who we really are through God's eyes, will we tear away false veils that shroud our identity in Him. God wants the full manifestation of Himself to be known in the earth. He wants His glory to shine, unhindered, through His likeness of male and female—He wants it released as reconciling love that heals hearts, families, and nations.

Over the past century, women have gained tremendous freedoms, but in myriad places around the world many have continued to suffer great intolerances. It's time for the daughters to be healed and rise in the power of the Holy Spirit.

This book is written for every woman, and is designed to touch every place where men and women meet in relationship, society, and faith. My intention is to show you the heart and purposes of God for you in the midst of what has often been termed as "a man's world"…and therein we see a misconception: this world isn't a man's world. It belongs to the Father. We are simply here to honor Him and steward what He gives us and where He places us.

I pray that the following pages will minister to your heart and show you the brilliant purpose of God for your life and the

18

permission, no, the charge of God, to engage it. The world needs women, as well as men, who are the manifest image of God for the healing of the nations. And it begins here, now, with you and me knowing our true identity in Christ as fully redeemed and empowered women of God.

- 1 -

GOOD-BYE,
SHRINKING VIOLET

"It's hard to fight an enemy who has outposts in your head."
— Sally Kempton

Life is a journey. An important part of this journey is coming to know who we are, and to understand the truth of our identity. After all, we are told so many things about our personhood through ideologies that range anywhere from appealing to appalling. These ideas come from our environment, upbringing, fashion, media, and religious training, or absence of it. For some, the journey of life is a delightful excursion of great discoveries. For others, it's been a search for freedom, perhaps even a desperate pursuit. Mine has been a mixture of both.

From early childhood, I felt an internal impulse of some divine purpose. However, these deep thoughts of destiny's voice were often met with a shadowy taunting that I could never fulfill such purpose because of one thing…my gender. I am female.

CULTURAL TIMIDITY TRAINING

I picked up on this message everywhere. Television programs often portrayed women's roles as subservient and their social display as timorous. From early on I was aware of women's limitations. Even if in subtle ways, a woman's voice didn't seem to carry as much value as a man's. If a wife wanted to do something she had to have permission, which to me, it didn't look much different than if she were a child.

Boys were free to dream of doing anything they wanted to. They were free to aspire to any career they chose. My traditional role, however, was more pre-determined, so higher education wasn't a necessity, though not withheld. When I was six, I was given a doll called "Shrinking Violet." You pulled her string and she said things like, "Hello, my name is Shrinking Violet...I'm afraid of noisy boys...Please, help me talk to people." Yes, timidity training started early!

I learned from Church culture that men could have certain gifts from God as spiritual leaders and teachers, but women could not. After all, the Bible says they are to be "silent." The underlying message I understood in all these things was clear: it was a man's world and my life, as a female, was somehow defined and limited. This echoed one huge message to me: purposelessness. I didn't mind the thought of being a wife under a man's rule as long as he loved me. But deep inside, I knew there was a purposeful destiny longing to be known, waiting to be discovered. I could feel its presence, like some brilliant intention uniquely mine from God just waiting for me to claim, if I dared.

But how could I dare? Was it permissible since I was of the female gender?

I know now that it was God Himself wanting to be known and His life liberated into my own. It was His presence I'd felt for so long calling me, but the bars of my cage obscured my vision and ability to respond.

22

I struggled against a world in which, as I perceived, females were viewed as second-class, less than, and not as valuable as males. Perhaps it was pride, but it bothered me. I wanted to feel valued. I didn't want to be what I secretly entertained as being "one of them"...but I was.

My mother was beautiful, refined, and worked in modeling in her younger years. But I mostly felt awkward and ugly. Growing up, I loved to climb trees, build forts and sit on roofs. I imagined myself as a pioneer and explorer of unchartered lands. I played "spy," made superhero outfits, crafted slingshots, made bows and arrows, and hit my brothers as needed. I even got into fist-fights with the neighborhood children...having two brothers just a year and two older than myself taught me survival basics.

Can you see now my challenge with cultural female boxes?

IDENTITY CRISIS

My internal conflict was fanned by a generation at odds with cultural norms. Society was outraged over our war in Vietnam, authority was rejected, anyone over thirty was mistrusted, and prayer was being removed from our schools. Drugs, "free love" and backstreet abortions were the new "thing." As the Civil Rights movement was finding its voice, so were women. Scenes of women burning their bras in public display, declaring freedom from gender-imposed limitations, are still imprinted on my brain today.

In 1969, just prior to my twelfth birthday, I experienced a deep encounter with Jesus' love and the presence of the Holy Spirit. This drew me into a burning passion for God's presence. It captivated me with a hunger for a freedom different from what I saw happening in culture, yet also unlike conventional church norms. I felt a crisis regarding who I was as a Christian girl.

The ideologies I sensed regarding the female role weren't a figment of my imagination. Studies made in the latter 1960s "showed the scholastic achievement of girls was higher in the early grades than in high school. The major reason given was that the girls' own expectations declined because neither their families nor their teachers expected them to prepare for a future other than that of marriage and motherhood. Traditionally, a middle-class girl in Western culture learned that cooking, cleaning, and caring for children was the behavior expected of her when she grew up."[1]

It was this absence of any other purpose or personal development that I perceived as prison walls. Without a doubt, Satan was also inciting and embellishing certain perceptions in my mind. I admit, too, at that point I wanted to be more than a housewife. Of course, when I later got married some of my views changed. I not only delighted in caring for our home and children, I counted it a privilege. I learned that raising children isn't merely changing diapers and sending them off to school, but about raising a nation's future leaders. I also developed personally as I raised our children, learning leadership, continuing my own education, and serving through missions, music ministry, and teaching. I learned that if I wanted my children to flourish in every way, I needed to flourish. I had to model what I desired them to live.

Today I know the truth of my identity as a godly woman, but I didn't know it growing up. And, unfortunately, the model that both encouraged and repressed me most wasn't the world, but religion.

CHRISTIAN FAMILY ORDER

In 1973, a training seminar for Christian families called *Basic Youth Conflicts Institute* gained national popularity. I was 15 at the time. Parents, hungry for an answer to the chaos of the 60's, flew by the droves with their children to hear the "wisdom" of this parenting expert. Thank God, an answer at last! Over the next few years, tens of thousands of people would fill stadiums from East to West to learn his secret to escaping the cultural madness tearing apart America's family structure.

My family joined the throng to receive this cutting-edge wisdom on family order. As my parents, two brothers and I entered the Portland Coliseum in Portland, Oregon, we were each handed a large red manual filled with diagrams and scriptures all explaining the proper place and attitude for each family member within family structure. Following the "plan" would ensure success as a family free from conflict.

My mom was especially hungry to know how to raise Christian children. She was prohibited from going to church when she was a child and this was the treasure house of wisdom she needed. Concepts were accompanied by a plethora of Bible verses...how could it be anything but good?

I remember sitting for hours listening to this man's intelligent discourse while marveling at his beautiful chalk drawings. However, it was the family diagram in my manual that troubled me. Deeply. On that page was a picture of a triangle at the top that represented God. Out of the triangle were arms extended forward, slightly bending inward at the elbows, with one hand holding a hammer, and the hammer was labeled "father." Positioned under the hammer was God's other hand holding a chisel labeled "mother," and under the chisel was a diamond labeled "child."

So here it was. My future place as a wife and mother would be under the blows of a man whose force I would channel to "shape" the child. My own position at that time in my life (as the child) was to receive the impact of a woman submitted to the force of a man. And it was God's own hand that was driving it!

As they say, a picture paints a thousand words...and I thought I was already having issues with gender roles!

It may not have been the intention of the instructor to suggest harsh hierarchal interaction as a "godly family structure," and, no doubt, there was some good in his materials that have helped many. However, the teaching tightened the chains of oppressive thinking both in my mind and in my mother's about our female role. For years I watched her trying to get my dad to "get with the program" as the family head. You know, be more forceful with discipline, lead the family in devotions, bring order to the chaos — while she tried to embrace a position of quiet subjection. And that was a problem for my mother whose fiery personality was anything but quiet! It was also a problem for my dad who was a laid-back and gentle man with a great sense of humor. He was a leader in business and ministry, but he was not a forceful man. Having married later in life after many years of military service, he left the home dynamics largely to my mother. And the teaching was certainly a problem for me — a confused, angry, diamond in the rough, waiting to be hammered into shape.

We were a family in conflict.

The message I perceived was that men were to be dominant and women were to be docile. Men were the leaders and women were to be quietly compliant. It seemed so "biblically" right, and left no question as to what a woman's "place" was. My mother and I both loved God. We weren't "Jezebels," nor had any desire to be. However, the structure felt rigid and lifeless, and lacked the one great dynamic we both hungered for as females — love and affirmation that make a woman flourish in the most nurturing environment intended by God: the family.

My conflict grew, hurling me into some very dark and turbulent years, until I experienced another intimate encounter with Jesus. I was 21 at the time. Spiritual bondage broke its hold as chains of addictions fell off me in the power of His presence. I had been crying out to Him for years, and was transformed in a moment in His glory. I saw Him. Then I understood my life from HIS perspective as a cherished bride with a purposeful destiny that I could dare to seize with Him.

That event ushered me into a new season of my life as I learned to experience life through His abiding love.

Truth handed me the personal worth I had longed for, along with a new horizon of great purpose. A few years later God gave me a loving husband, along with spiritual fathers who didn't limit me because of my gender, but saw me as a fellow heir and laborer in the Kingdom.

Over the next twenty years, I flourished in family living, life, and ministry. Nevertheless, there were still some areas in my thinking incongruent with His—areas still trapped in shades of falsehoods where He wanted to shine His light. There was more divine work to be done in me as a woman on a walk with God. He wanted to take me into new realms of Kingdom advancement, but He knew that I would not be able to move with Him until my limiting mindsets were addressed with truth.

ENCOUNTER WITH FATHER

In late 1999, I experienced a deep encounter with Abba Father that revolutionized my life in a new way, especially regarding my identity as His *daughter*! I've discovered that my life in Christ is one of continual and transforming revelation of God. A reoccurring circumstance, outside my control, presented itself again, but this time a sense of rejection climaxed to an explosive moment...I had a meltdown. I felt completely undone and every remnant of feeling worthless—not to God, but in the opinion of certain people—surfaced in overwhelming pain. It was like every unhealed heart wound from conception till then had surfaced in critical mass.

I had worked hard at keeping my heart clean from unforgiveness toward others, but it was the feelings of rejection and lack of value I'd experienced through life that I had continued to suppress, "stuff," and internalize without realizing it. Like an infection, it had festered far beneath the surface. The current event was simply the last straw.

Then came Father.

Words elude me in picturing for you what He did—or rather, how He did it—but the power of His intimate presence pulled me out of a black abyss of lostness in an area of my identity that I didn't know still existed. He not only cleansed and healed those deep wounds, but anchored me in a new level of divine affirmation and validation. And there was more—there was a new element He awakened in me...His authority.

Until that moment, I knew who I was in God, but I didn't know who I was. Does that make sense? I had lived in the knowledge of being Christ's bride as a pure and godly woman, doing the right things, and making the right choices, making Him my priority in everything. Nevertheless, there was more that God wanted me to walk in.

It was time to step into a new place of knowing my identity as the Father's daughter with authority for Kingdom advancement in a way I had not walked in before. Certainly not as a domineering female, but as a woman in unison with the Holy Spirit, doing the Father's will, undaunted, undeterred, and in burning love.

For this new place, I could not be sunk or swayed by the opinions or affirmation of people. I could not live as a people-pleaser. This required a new realm of intimate confidence in who Jesus is in me and who I am in Him. It necessitated a new level of vision unhindered by limiting mindsets. It called for a new depth of intimacy with God that anchors the soul in His opinion alone.

In those hours of encounter, the remaining hidden web of self-rejection melted away. From there, God took me into a season of daily learning His name more intimately. Not only do I celebrate my womanhood in a new way, but I celebrate my sisters worldwide in a new way, too. I see the divine purpose they carry, as well as the delight that Father has in them.

Today, I delight to be a part of "one of them."

I used to think I was alone in my gender issues. However, as I've voiced my journey to others, I have met women everywhere having experienced the same struggle. Women long to break free of glass ceilings and rise empowered into their God-designed potential and place, yet with a right spirit. It's part of who we are as a new creation in Christ.

God wants women set free in His love, affirmed in His truth, with power to rise in divine purpose with Him.

I threw away my Shrinking Violet years ago and all the fearful and limiting declarations that went with her. Today, I dare to seize my destiny with Christ to its fullest, joining Jesus in His stride to release the Father's Kingdom on earth. And the banner He has put in my hand, for one, is the government of His love to restore women to their divine design.

This restoration must take place in order for the entire body and Bride of Christ to rise, in this hour, for the healing of homes, cultures, and nations.

LET MY DAUGHTERS GO

In June of 2011, I was invited to speak at a women's conference in Dallas, TX, to be held later that year. The topic I was given was *Understanding Your Identity in Christ*. The conference would include women from every denomination, and having been in church culture all my life, I knew this subject to be one of the most important, yet least grasped, in the body of Christ—for both men and women.

At the time, I was working as a medical assistant, helping to put our kids through college. I was also busy with ministry and writing my third book, *Heaven's Secret of Success*. A month prior to the conference, my manuscript was off to print and I was able to settle down and focus on what Father wanted to say to His daughters. I thought I knew, at least in part, what I would teach, but what God began to show me was something more than what I'd ever seen before. Something greater...and His message was loud and clear: "Let My daughters go!"

As I dug deep into the Word, my celebration and understanding of our identity as women went to a whole new level. I had lived for years in the experience of New Testament redemption, but oh the wonders that He was now showing me of our intimate creation from the beginning was overwhelming! I remembered a book that a Bible Professor had given me some years previous called, *God's Word for Women* by Dr. Katharine Bushnell. As I leafed through its pages, it confirmed things the Holy Spirit was showing me in Scripture.

When the conference date arrived, I was excited about the fresh word God had given me — it was like "new wine" bubbling in my spirit. The church facility was fairly large and speakers came from many places. As I set up my book table before the opening session, I also felt a certain tension. I knew I was facing differing views on the topic of women. I just didn't know how big a religious toe I was about to step on!

MEETING GOLIATH

The leaders gathered for prayer, and we committed the day to the Lord, praying for lives changed and women set free. As I made my way to my assigned room where I would teach my *"fresh revelation hot off the press,"* I was aware of a dark presence. I knew it was spiritual warfare so I continued to pray as I prepared to speak.

The women in my first workshop leaned in with interest as I shared from the Word and my own journey. For some, you could see the chains of oppression falling off them. Afterward, a group of five women, including a pastor's wife, came up to me with tears. They related how they were from out of town and their conversation in the hotel room, just the night before, had been on the very topic I had taught. Deep questions they'd had for years involving their role and struggle as women in church culture had finally found an answer. Others, too, thanked me for fresh understanding of God's intentions toward them as women.

30

As the next session began, I again asked the Lord to let His voice be heard. This was, after all, a message of freedom, empowerment, and affirmation from *Him* to His daughters. Sometimes, however, "empowerment" and "women" are incongruous terms in religious settings. To support such words can be equivalent to inciting female rebellion, giving place to a Jezebel spirit, or enlisting women into some kind of Christian feminist army! I was aware that my audience carried diverse doctrines, some celebrating women's spiritual gifts (including leadership), while others forbidding it.

While I was not there to promote any riotous notion—nope, not even a "spiritual bra burning"—I was there to relay from heaven their original design, full redemption, and restored authority in Christ. I knew this *new wine* would not fit into some of their *wine skins*, but I had to give what Father gave me to minister.

Growing up, my family attended about every denomination in town from Presbyterian to Church of Christ to Baptist to Pentecostal to Assembly of God, and more. My parents were spiritually hungry, searching for the presence of God...they just had a hard time sometimes finding Him in Church! I was aware of the diverse and even dividing beliefs that pervade in Christendom.

The following day I received the written feedback from the classes. Comments ranged anywhere from "fantastic" and "great biblical understanding" to "it *felt* unbiblical" and "check your speakers!" I was a little taken back at the word "unbiblical" since I am careful to draw teachings from Scripture with Hebrew and Greek root meaning. I have a high standard for Christian teachers, including myself, to be sound and congruent with God's meaning in what He wrote. Every one of us wants proper representation— so does God!

As I prayed, I realized that it wasn't my teaching that was unbiblical. The key word in the comment was that it *"felt"* unbiblical. Ideologies that we've embraced can sometimes *feel* truer than the truth itself...just as limiting mindsets can often feel *safe*, if they've been our accustomed norm. To live in truth requires trusting God's words over our own opinions or that of others, including what a leader may have taught us. Honored leaders are human, too. Not one of us is above error.

Living in truth often means daring to cross into a new way of doing things, perhaps foreign to how we've done things before...including the risk of being labeled "wrong" by esteemed brothers and sisters.

I don't discount that perhaps my teaching could have been more polished as I presented this fresh insight on identity. I am learning that new understanding often needs to settle awhile, allowing the Holy Spirit to continue to unfold and deepen it in my spirit before sharing it. However, I am also well acquainted with teachings that use the judgment paradigm of the Fall to teach a redeemed woman her place!

Any doctrine that negates a woman's full redemption is an affront to the cross and resurrection of Jesus Christ. It denies the power of His blood to fully restore our identity in God and cleanse us from every stain of sin. Such doctrines are fueled by the same religious spirit that Jesus dealt with in His days on earth...a spirit that He said, "...shuts out the Kingdom of heaven."

Days after the conference, I still felt the threatening loom of *Goliath's* presence. I knew I'd come up against a powerful stronghold in Christendom of traditional doctrine regarding women. The temptation to say *'I'll never teach that again'* was overwhelming. But that was exactly what the enemy wanted me to do.

I shared this with my friend who had coordinated the event. She affirmed how I felt. However, tossing aside my excuses of why I didn't want to "go there" again, she emphasized, "Nicole, you have a message to speak and women need to hear it! You can't let the enemy win." I knew she was right. Nevertheless, I didn't want to step into the arena with that strongman again, at least for a while.

THE FATHER'S MESSAGE

Three months later, I was asked to speak to a women's group — again, on a woman's identity in Christ. I accepted. After the meeting, a seventeen-year-old girl approached me saying that my message had changed her life. She had heard me at the conference a few months earlier and now again. She shared how she, too, had struggled with understanding her place as a young Christian woman. She also felt destiny beating in her heart, but the voice of legalism within the Church had tried to convince her that her passion was forbidden territory. I knew then that this message wasn't just to older women, but to the younger generation as well.

As she hugged me and moved away, another woman stepped forward and remarked, "You know, what you are teaching is right, but it's really more for a man to say these things regarding a woman's place." In that moment, a part of me wanted to agree and apologize for my daring words. I thought how much easier it would be to wait for a man to speak up for a woman's full redemption. I could avoid the risk of being branded a "feminist." I could evade the discomfort in some who'd rather sweep the woman's journey under the rug and hang on to tradition. After all, we've done it for centuries. But we can't do that anymore.

The Holy Spirit is moving and He doesn't want to be restrained by structures that He did not design! The Father has a world He wants to heal! He needs His sons and daughters to join Him.

Though tempted again to relinquish my voice, I also knew this wasn't "my" message. Father is calling His children, both male *and* female, to rise with Him in doing the work He's called us to do. Many women do not rise to their full calling in God because they don't know how, or what that looks like…or that they have permission to do so. However, there is a fresh move of the Holy Spirit upon women today and Father is removing false structures that have limited His daughters. It's time for us, together with our brothers, to be the display of God's wisdom in the earth.

ANSWERING THE FATHER'S CALL

A few months after that event I was in a worship service when the Lord spoke this to my spirit: "Where My people embrace the concept of a silenced and disempowered woman, they will embrace the concept of a silent and disempowered Bride of Christ. It's time for women and the Church to know their identity in Me!"

Jesus' Bride on earth (the true Church) is not to be silent or powerless. Women in Christ, alongside men in Christ, must know who they are in Him in this hour. Jesus is calling us to rise, as sons of God and as Christ's Bride, to walk with Him in the full power of the Spirit.

For some, this message of empowerment in Christ will be new. For many it will be wonderfully liberating. For others it will be continued confirmation of what the Holy Spirit has already been showing you. The Father says it's time to know our identity in Him. The soul of our society languishes in darkness and in need of healing. The nations worldwide are in need of spiritual fathers and mothers with heaven's counsel in their mouth, divine authority in their words, and healing in their hands. We are here for such a time as this.

We must not be silent. We must throw away our Shrinking Violets.

Today, we are in a spiritual war against the knowledge of God and His image in gender. As the body of Christ we must reconcile in the unity of the Spirit and in the truth of our identity in Him. In the pages ahead, you will see that our battles are not with mere flesh and blood, whether a person, a social behavior, or doctrine. Identity, including gender identity, is a *spiritual matter*.

34

There is only One who can define that identity in truth for us, and in His truth, we are free...free to soar on wings of destiny and dignity as our Father's sons and daughters.

You are a woman designed by God. He calls you to come away with Him and step into His fullness for your life. For this, you must know the truth of how He laced His own likeness into your very gender from the beginning. Come with me and let's look now at how God brilliantly fashioned male and female as His glorious image on earth.

- 2 -

A BRILLIANT BEGINNING

"The beginning is the most important part of the work."
— Plato

I once heard that to train an elephant to stay put, you begin when it's a baby by chaining its foot to a post. When it's older, all you have to do is use a light rope and it won't run off. It has learned its limitation. It has internalized through experience what it can or cannot do...even though it would only take a simple tug on the rope to walk out its freedom.

No doubt most of us have felt personal limitations because of experience, environments, and teaching. Some of those limitations are real, some are perceived, but both can hold us back. Jesus said that to abide in His words is to live in truth, and that truth will set us free. The elephant may never find out the truth of its great power and ability to walk free, but we can.

The truth about our identity is rooted in our Creator who made us in His image. We've grown up looking to the world, positions, peers and leaders to give us our identity, hoping they would celebrate our existence, affirm our value, and explain our purpose. And some do. But even at best, most will fail us in some way, tying us to the post of their limited understanding. As Paul said, we only know in part. I'm grateful for my parents and the godly leaders God has put in my life through the years, but I've learned by experience that the only sure foundation any of us can completely rely on is God's unwavering, unfailing, unalterable truth. His Word is truth. His Word holds the truth about our identity.

Because of the Fall, the dignity of human identity has often been misunderstood, misinterpreted, and misrepresented. At a glance, creation seems to be a basic story of God forming a man and a woman. But in looking closer, using the lens of the Hebrew language (the original language of Genesis), we see a marvelous pattern of divine purpose woven into the fabric of male and female in God's image. Psalm 139 beautifully describes how a person's physical attributes are knit together in their mother's womb. Likewise, at creation, God knit together distinctive qualities to form, not just the physical attributes of humanity, but the very nature of their spirit and soul in His likeness.

While letters of the English language denote merely sound, Hebrew is a spiritual language with every letter expressed through pictures that open to us a vault of divine knowledge. And what's more, each letter has a numerical value that adds to the wealth of hidden revelation. Hebrew is a language that God chose to use in revealing Himself to us, so that in seeing Him, we will also know our own identity and purpose in Him.

Hebrew is also a *covenant* language. Thus, in looking at our creation we must view it through the framework of *covenant relationship*, that being, an intimate agreement initiated by God with mankind. And though the first Adam broke covenant with God (which we will see), a new covenant is given us through the Last Adam, Jesus Christ. We cannot know God apart from covenant intimacy; we can only know about Him. But God wants us to know Him...intimately.

As we journey through the intricate design of creation language, I encourage you to ask the Holy Spirit — the Teacher — to help you breathe in the beauty of the fabric from which you have been woven as a woman. As we explore the richness of God's work in humanity, I want you to see three important things that will be like a golden thread throughout this book:

1. The image of God is expressed through *both* male and female gender
2. The husband-wife union is a portrait of Christ and His Bride (Body)
3. The empowered redeemed woman is a portrait of Christ's Bride

Being an empowered woman isn't about being domineering, arrogant or pushy. It is about being who God made you to be in Christ without fear, timidity, or limiting beliefs. It's about flourishing in life, naturally and spiritually, and the charge of God to do so!

God has given you many gifts from Him, and one of them is your gender. It's not an albatross around your neck or a curse as some suppose. It is not the result of "bad karma" or some evil you did in a "past life." It doesn't make you second-class or "less than" a man, no matter what another's personal viewpoint is. Your Father's perspective is the one you are to live by. Womanhood is a gift of God's image given to you and is meant to shine with His glory and dignity.

So, here we go. Open your heart as we explore some amazing and empowering details. As they say, knowledge is power! You are meant for a life of power as a woman of influence and carrier of divine presence. I am aware that looking at the etymology of words can, at times, seem tedious. So please bear with me over these next two chapters as they are full of critical and foundational truths for knowing our identity, as defined by our Creator. I pray for the Spirit of revelation over you as we look into the hidden mysteries of a woman's original design.

GOD BEGINS WITH A MAN

Everything we see begins with the Creator, so we are going to look at where He began when fashioning a woman—He started with a man, a man in His own image. It's honoring to appreciate a man's true identity as we endeavor to know our own. After all, he was the first part of God's revealed image. She was the next part, the completing part, as you will see.

As we embark on our journey, I admit my struggle in writing this chapter on the man and woman at creation. I cut and pasted multiple times, trying to find a unified, yet individual flow, to my presentation. It wasn't until I finally printed the pages and laid them in a row that I clearly understood my dilemma. And then I fell to my knees, overwhelmed with the wonder of God! He so intricately entwined the revelation of Himself in male and female gender, sharing certain qualities equally, yet making each so unique, that it was like having to take a surgeon's knife to separate their fine details while holding to their unity. With that said, I ask for your patience as I do my best to unfold for you what I've so wonderfully discovered.

Let's look now at the divine story of God and man:

God said, "Let US make man [Adam] in OUR image, according to OUR likeness: and let *them* rule…. God created man in His own image, in the image of God created He him; male and female created He them… God blessed them; and God said to them, 'Be fruitful and multiply, and fill the earth, and subdue it; and rule'… then the LORD God formed man of dust from the ground, and breathed into his nostrils the breath of life; and man became a living being. The LORD God planted a garden toward the east, in Eden; and there He placed the man whom He had formed…. Then the LORD God said, 'It is not good for the man to be alone; I will make him a helper suitable for him.' So the LORD God caused a deep sleep to fall upon the man, and he slept; then He

40

took one of his ribs and closed up the flesh at that place. The LORD God fashioned into a woman the rib which He had taken from the man, and brought her to the man... and God called *their* name Adam, in the day when they were created." (Gen. 1:26-27 KJV; Gen. 2:7,8, 18, 21-22, 5:1b-2 NASB, clarification mine)

The glorious *"US"* was the Divine Creator, *Elohim*: the Father, Son, and Holy Spirit. God, inspired by a most audacious thought, used the blueprint of Himself to form a being in His own likeness.

In Genesis 2, we glimpse the Master Potter at work. Carefully He gathers some dust from the ground, using it as clay to form a human being. As I close my eyes and imagine this scene, I envision God bending intently over His masterpiece — every touch of the divine hand infusing bold imprints of love, goodness, and strength. Then, dipping His large hand deep into luminescent bowls of mercy and compassion, He weaves these into the core of His child. And when finished, He puts His face intimately to the face of the man and breathes into him the breath of life...and God's image on earth comes fully alive!

There he stood, the son of Love and offspring of Light, unique from every other creature. Lifting His son into His arms, Father God took him to the place specially prepared for him — the Garden called Eden, which means, "Delight!" Then, bursting into song as angels accompanied with heavenly harmonies, *Elohim* danced joyfully with THEIR son. Then God appointed His image the task of cultivating and guarding this garden territory.

The man would be the *protector, ruler, and husbandman* to ensure that all was delightfully well in the land beneath his rule. He was the Father's *watchman* and *governing authority to prosper its wellbeing.* He was, you could say, Father's apostle to minister heaven's culture on earth.

The animals came to him without fear. As their governor, he named them one by one, each name reflecting their nature and character. God instructed His son that he could freely enjoy the

41

fruit of every tree, except one — the tree of the knowledge of good and evil that stood in the middle of the garden, next to the tree of life. God came every day to talk with the son who bore His likeness...and his name was Adam.

THE FIRST ADAM

The Hebrew word for *Adam* means: *man* or *mankind* (human race). While it is often used only in referring to this first man, God also used it in referring to the woman: *"and God called **their** name Adam, in the day when they were created"* (Gen. 5:1). That's right, God didn't call them Adam and Eve, He called *them* Adam.

To name something is to give it an identity. God identified them both as Adam. Eve was a name given by the man after the Fall, when their unity had been broken.

"Adam" **consists of three Hebrew picture letters: Aleph, Dalet, Mem.**[1]

- *Aleph* means "ox" and speaks of being first, leader, and strength
- *Dalet* means door, passageway or access
- *Mem* means water, liquid, or even chaos

These picture letters described Adam as a *strong leader.* Hebrew references also describe Adam as *"first blood."*[2] Adam was God's son, a carrier of covenant (the Edenic covenant[3]). This supplied Adam with free access to God's presence and divine provision for himself and the territory where God placed him. He was the *gateway* and *path* for connecting heaven's supply to earth's needs.

Now all this applied to the woman too! As Adam, she was a *strong leader* and *first blood* because she was taken from the man's DNA. Remember, God saw them as one, calling them both "Adam." We must see this aspect of gender unity as it pictures how the Father sees us as one in kind and quality. It is also how

He sees us in Christ as one with His Son, being in Him and from His DNA ("as He is, so are we," 1 John 4:17).

Remember what I said, that all through this book you will see your identity as a woman and how it parallels the identity of Christ's Bride in the earth—one that has also suffered many false identities. There is such a deep mystery in creation, one so divine that earthly words fail to sufficiently describe. It's like hearing a heavenly melody and trying to sing it with earth's limited tones.

Being *first blood* made mankind's blood different than an animal's blood, including the fact that our blood has a "voice" when it's shed (Gen 4:10). Shedding the life of one created in God's image carries great consequence and effect in the earth.

THE PROTECTOR

In this simple record of creation, we see many key elements to a man's grand design, two of these being that he was the son of Love, and he was to guard and cultivate territory. In fact, throughout creation this territorial design is seen in much of *paternal* nature—bucks that defend realms, bulls that vie for dominance and boys that fight for preeminence, and for what they consider as belonging to them.

Protecting is a spiritual design that God has put into males for the purpose of righteous governing. This also links with their design as watchmen to keep an environment safe and prospering!

For those of you with sons or young men under your guidance, when you see this territorial character come alive at puberty (some of us call it "sprouting horns"…in more ways than one), help them to understand this nature as part of their God-given identity to do good, and not for harm. Their strength and sense of territory is given for *appropriate* protecting, and not for bullying or hurting others.

As you teach them to seek the Father's purpose for their life, the commission to guard and cultivate a sphere of influence will be an important part of it. They will have to learn how to use their gift for God's designs in God's way—to lift others up, serve and prosper them, and not oppress them.

Most of us are aware of *territorial spirits* as demonic forces that preside over cities and nations. But too often we haven't understood that our Heavenly Father is territorial too!

"The earth is His and all it contains."
(Psalm 24:1)

Psalm 115:16 says, *"The heavens are the heavens of the Lord, but the earth He has given to the sons of men."* Family, community, and nations are territory, and He has wired men especially for the *physical* protecting of territory.

It is the design of rulers to protect. It is also their charge from God to make the land fruitful and prosperous.

Men need to know their identity as God's image, just like women do. Knowing the place of honor that they carry as the paternal likeness of God is key to their prosperity. When men don't know their true identity in God, the strength and nature given them is vulnerable to being displayed through harmful and even evil acts.

Men are endued with physical strength and a strategic ability to wage war, which equips them as the defender-protectors of land and family. Women (being from the man), also have a protective nature, though our part looks a little different. We will look at our part more in a moment, but here I want to emphasize the rich design of a man.

THE FLAMING HAND OF POWER

In Genesis 2:23-24, we see another Hebrew word for *man:"Iysh."*

"She shall be called woman [Ishshah], because she was taken out of man [Iysh]. For this reason a man [Isyh] shall leave his father and his mother, and be joined to his wife [Ishshah]; and they shall become one flesh."

"*Iysh*" and "*Ishshah*" give us an even deeper insight into the unity, yet individuality, of God's image in them. It also reflects covenant relationship since these words were used when the man acknowledged her design, and received her in likeness of himself for marriage. Let's look at what *Iysh* means first.

The Hebrew picture letters for *Iysh* are: Aleph, Yod, Shin.[4]

- *Aleph* pictures an "ox" signifying: first, leader, strength
- *Yod* is a "hand" signifying: a strong arm, power, work
- *Shin* is "teeth" meaning: what consumes, destroys, breaks down, overcomes; the letter *Shin* also carries three points of flame

First, again we see him as a **strong leader**. He was also an **overcomer**.

Second, two of these letters together (*Aleph* and *Shin*) form the Hebrew word "fire" (*"esh"*) showing that he carried an *internal spiritual fire* as God's likeness, for God is a Consuming Fire (Heb. 12:29).

Fire is energy, light, and power and speaks to us of the divine light put in man's spirit to unify him with God and energize him for action in divine work. Mankind's design is to host the perpetual fire of God — the burning flame of His presence that illumines, purifies, and empowers growth, direction and momentum for accomplishing the works of God.

In Revelation 1, we see the Last Adam, Jesus, whose eyes are as a flame of fire and His feet as burnished bronze. This is a picture of the entire life set aflame, illumined, and energized by the Holy Spirit to be a "burning one." In other words, all lights on and fully engaged with God — the opposite of a flickering, dim, or smoldering lamp.

Third, the letter *Yod* (the hand and strong arm) is unique to the man at creation. It is a *symbol of power*, giving him that *double endowment of strength and ability to protect, provide, and cultivate territory*. This power nature is why guys gravitate to things like building muscle, power tools, fast cars, heavy machines, and rough sports. It's why boys like to play with "power" toys and building sets and why they love things that explode and make noise. Men were made for power — to lift heavy weights or burdens, to fight, win, and overcome. It's part of God's nature...when used in the right way.

GOD'S POINT MAN

The Hebrew letter *Yod* also defines the man as being *"a divine point of energy."* One resource puts it like this: "The *Yod* is considered the starting point of the presence of God in all things...as the *'spark'* of the Spirit...yet being the smallest of the Hebrew letters it also speaks of *humility*.... The *Yod* is the first letter of the Divine Name *Yahweh* and of *Yeshua*, and indicates its preeminence.[5]

The man was created as God's *point man*: the beginning and spark of divine power for what bears God's presence in the earth. He was created as *God's catalyst* for fruitfulness in divine work and family, giving him an honorable place of *preeminence.* And yet, this work wasn't designed to be with pride, dominance or control, but with the impulse of divine love and humility as reflected in the size of the *Yod*.

As a woman, I have been blessed with a marriage to a man who has truly been the *Yod* of God to me. His love has been the catalyst of a beautiful marriage, and has made me flourish as a woman in every way. His protection and care have lifted me into a fruitful destiny both inside and outside the home. He has never suppressed, repressed or harmed me. And in response to his tender love, I honor him. I esteem who he is. I respect his words because I know that he never tries to control me, but to help and empower me.

I don't talk ugly to him, demean him, or try to manipulate him with my emotions. But, I admit, I've had to learn these things over the years by listening to the Holy Spirit in dealing with my attitudes, emotions, and motives...and especially the way I communicate. I've had to grow in self-control, to lasso my frustrations and fears into a place of peace as I walk with God in my relationships. Women are communicators and our words can be as much a dagger as a man's hand can act like a hammer. We both have to learn to submit our strengths, as well as weaknesses, to God.

God's greatest leaders throughout history were men of strength *and* humility: Abraham, Moses, David, and the greatest of all—Jesus, God's Son. He humbled Himself to the death of the cross, destroying the power of sin and death on our behalf. This gave Him preeminence and a name above all names. He is God's *Starting Point* for us, and for all the children of God who embrace His New Covenant.

Since men are God's starting points for family, they play a huge role in the healing of families, and thus in the healing of culture and nations. The assault we are seeing in America today on marriage, gender, and family is a strategic spiritual attack on God's image in humanity.

The key words for the man's design are: **protector, power,** and **preeminence.** The man was created a ruler over a specific domain as a humble bearer of God's presence and government...a government of LOVE. He was the image of the paternal nature of God as a catalyst and protector of life.

As I mentioned before, Hebrew letters are not only pictorial, but carry numeric significance. The numeric meaning of *Iysh* is: **unity** (Aleph—1), **divine order** and **completion** (Yod—10), and **atonement** and **reconciliation** (Shin—300, which relates to covenant).[6] Atonement is the agreement and reconciliation that results when a controversy is satisfied by the giving of an equivalent for an offense or injury.[7]

These values describe the man as being in union with God to minister reconciliation of all that was under his care, aligning it

47

with heaven's design (order). The man was a king, bearing God's government, as well as a priest over his appointed territory.

How much the world needs men to be in unity with God! To be spiritual fathers and leaders who reconcile issues with God's heart and ways, bringing alignment with heaven for prosperity of life and divine purpose. Men, in link with God, hold a powerful place to release the designs of God into culture and lift others into divine destiny.

We need to celebrate and esteem how God created men. As women, we must encourage them with life giving words, and pray for their rise into divine calling and identity. The world is looking for men to shine in the light of authentic design as the display of God's true paternal nature in the earth—especially in the midst of today's cultures that are being fueled by the energy of false designs.

HOME ALONE

The man, however, could not fully prosper alone in what God had called him to do. He could not be fruitful alone, or increase alone, or even fully rule alone. Observing His son, God declared, *"It is not good that man should be alone"* (Gen. 2:18). The word "alone" (Heb. *"bad"*) means: separation, a part, something apart. The man was only "a part" of God's image; he wasn't the whole of it. It was time for the other part!

It was time to complete the picture of God's revealed image on earth. It was time for the woman to come forth! Taking a rib from the royal watchman, *Elohim* used it to fashion another person—the other part of His likeness.

God is neither male nor female, but in Him are both natures. God reveals Himself to us as our Father and the Initiator of life. He is the beginning of all things and so we refer to Him as "He," but He is also called *El Shaddai: "the many breasted One"* who is completely nourishing, satisfying, and supplies His people with

48

all their needs as a mother would her child. God not only gives life, but He sustains life. Thus, within Him are both the paternal and maternal characteristics.

Part of carrying God's likeness is our internal design for relationship and community. God Himself is relational as a Holy Community of Three in One. He designed family as the reflection of Himself to be a safe, relational, intimate, community—a family "unit."

We see this design for unity reflected in how Jesus calls us His "Body"—many *parts* rightly *joined together* with Him as the Head.

Scientific studies have even shown that a human baby will actually die if deprived of human touch, in spite of it having sufficient warmth and food. We need the loving embrace of friends and family. God designed that you and I flourish best in right relationships. We were not designed to live or prosper alone...just as the man, who being in a place of *apartness*, could not fully prosper as God intended.

THE COMPLETER

Some have tried to interpret the woman's "later arrival" as making her lesser in importance or even quality, but we will continue to see that this is not God's perspective. Every aspect of God's likeness is to be cherished. Remember, God made animals before man, so the sequence of creation doesn't suggest that animals are better than man, or that a man is better than a woman. Rather, all progression in creation prepared an environment for the next revelation of God and His work. You will see why I mention these things later, as we hold cultural philosophies to the light of God's truth.

It's one thing to embark on a purposeful journey; it's another thing to finish it...both elements are needed. Starting and finishing are important dynamics to God's designs. He started with a man, but finished with a woman.

"For I am confident of this very thing, that He who began a good work in you will perfect it until the day of Christ Jesus" (Phil. 1:6).

I like to think that the woman was the icing on the cake, the cherry on top, and the crowning jewel of God's creation. She was the last Christmas package under the creation tree. No less valuable, but presented in the right time when Father wanted to unveil His glorious daughter, the bride. I also like to think of the time lapse between the man and woman as being the lingering, yet proud, stride of the Father walking His daughter down the aisle.

She was not an afterthought (as some have taught through the centuries). The timing of her appearance was not an accident, but was a divine statement on so many levels. She was a *forethought* in God's heart from before the foundations of the world. He didn't fashion her as an, "Oops, I forgot. Sorry you're lonely, here you go." The woman was *in* the man, and then was fashioned *from* him...intentionally. Both were created to reveal the likeness of God. She *completed* His work of creation.

God certainly could have created male and female humans at the same time, and in the same way, as He did other creatures. However, He didn't for a reason. He was the Master Designer painting an exquisite portrait of divine truth.

God put the first Adam into a deep sleep, just as the Father put His Son, the Last Adam, into the sleep of death on the cross for His Bride to come forth. And just as the first daughter was fashioned with the son's DNA to reign over earth with him, so the Bride of Christ is fashioned with Christ's DNA as a co-heir and ruler with Him (2 Tim. 2:12).

Using the rib from the man, *Elohim* fashioned the woman. Carefully He wove into her tender form the essence of His gentleness and endurance, pouring in an extra measure of kindness as well as courage. His strong hand imprinted into her being the signet likeness of Himself, just as He had with the man. She was the revelation of God's maternal attributes. She completed the picture of His likeness in humanity.

Together the man and woman would rule as the image of God, protecting the garden, causing it to flourish, and parenting future generations in the intimate knowledge of *Elohim*...and they would live happily ever after....

THE BRIDE

I love to think about what her first moments with the Creator might have been like before the man opened his eyes. What words may have been shared between Father and daughter before He walked her down the path to His son...to the one who would be her husband. The man had his own "alone time" with Father before she appeared. She too had her "alone time" before the man awoke.

Alone time in God's presence is an important part of our life as His sons and daughters.

The man identified the woman as being part of himself (bone of his bone) and embraced her to be his wife, his bride. The word *"bride"* (Heb. *"kallah"*) means: to complete, finished of a work, fulfilled in regards to purpose or prediction of, bring to an end, finish doing a thing, fulfill, bring to pass, accomplished, enclose. She not only completed the revelation of God's image in earthly form, but she completed the man as a co-laborer in the purposes of God.

Completing was wired into the woman in many ways, including the ability to give a human life a nurturing environment to grow and develop fully. A woman stands as one created in God's likeness to help bring divine purpose to full maturity. Perhaps this completing nature is also one of the reasons why we, as women, so often look for closure in situations. We don't like

51

things just dangling or unresolved issues, especially in relationships. Marriage itself is a form of *closure* in a relationship—the final uniting of two separate lives to become as one through covenant. This is counter to much of today's culture that often lacks the closure of committed love.

ISHSHAH, THE FIERY REVELATOR

We have already seen what the name *Adam* meant for both the male and female, and the Hebrew significance of "*Iysh.*" Now let's look at the word "*Ishshah*" for her.

The Hebrew picture letters for *Ishshah* are: Aleph, Shin, Hey. [8]

- *Aleph* pictures an "ox" signifying: first, leader, strength
- *Shin* is "teeth" meaning: what consumes, destroys, breaks down, overcomes
- *Hey* pictures someone standing with arms open wide looking upward. It means: look, behold!, window, divine breath, revelation, light

Do you remember the letters we discussed for *Iysh (man)*? Two Hebrew letters for *Ishshah* are the same as for *Iysh: Aleph* and *Shin.* She too, was a **strong leader** and **overcomer**. She too hosted the presence of **holy fire** within her spirit. Again, this is important for us because many women grow up thinking: *I'm not a leader!* But the truth is that we were designed to lead alongside men.

It may not sound right to some due to certain religious training, **but God's image is leadership—male and female.** This is why we see Jesus lifting His Bride to sit with Him in heavenly places, giving her authority and ruling power. This isn't my opinion; it's God's Word. Your leadership may look different than someone else's, because of your personality, temperament, motivational gifts and leadership style. And too, some have stronger leadership gifts than others. But lead, you must—by your spirit, attitude, voice, influence, position, passions, and gifts.

Women are often taught to only be followers, but this teaches us to be passive, powerless, shutdown, and do what we're told — even perhaps unquestionably. It limits us in how we think and act. It makes us dim rather than living as burning ones. Like I said, this doesn't mean we are to be "Jezebels," but it does mean we must have a mindset of active leadership in this world.

We were designed to rule. This means we must be pro-active to mentor, lead, and teach. As we experience intimacy with God, we learn to immerse our sphere of influence in the knowledge of Him, and display His good works. We are fashioned with His image to act with divine strategy, courage, and wisdom. We were NOT designed to be passive or intimidated.

Women, like men, were created to be energized by the Holy Spirit for righteous action with pure motives. Such holy fire is never to be quenched or snuffed out!

THE COMMUNICATOR

While the man's uniqueness is the *Yod*, God gave the woman her own special quality — the letter "*Hey*." The *Hey* is the portrait of a window that gives the ability to peer beyond an enclosure, a window that opens to the atmosphere of a world beyond. It is also a picture of one who stands beholding heaven, breathing in the revelation of God and releasing it on earth.

One resource says this: "It is said that the breath of God's mouth refers to the sound of the letter *Hey* — the breathing out of the Spirit."[9]

God designed the woman to see Him, to breathe in the dynamic life of His voice, and to release His words into this world as a helper in His likeness (we will see more of this nature in the next chapter). She was fashioned to *experience* God, to feel the warmth of His intimate love, and sense the movement of the Spirit on her face. Her design was woven with the capacity to engage with God in a world beyond earth's enclosures.

She reflected the maternal nature of the Spirit of God who is the Comforter and Teacher. She stood regal in her beauty as one specifically designed, of all things, to have a voice! And since the Fall, it's the one thing that has been most twisted, altered, and silenced! Nevertheless, we will see her voice fully redeemed in Christ.

Many women around the world have struggled greatly in being made to feel that they do not have a voice – that they are to be silent. But this was never God's design for a woman! The female Adam was the embodiment of God's creative power in speech that releases divine purpose! I want to tell you that Father has given us permission in the Son to cast off the chains of silence and proclaim what He says. The likeness of God is not in being mute! We will clarify in later chapters what God's Word truly says about women in regards to teaching and speaking.

Speaking is one of our authentic designs. We just have to learn to use it in harmony with the Holy Spirit! Revelation 22 says, "The Spirit and the Bride SAY...!" The problem at the Fall was speaking in alignment with God's enemy that brought destruction.

This gift of communication made the woman a powerful influencer. It's a no-brainer to say that girls like to communicate. When girls get together, the room is abuzz with chatter and laughter. I'm always pulling my husband into active discussion over the day's events, plans for tomorrow, and whatever I can think of! I like to connect and verbally interact.

This nature is noticeable from early on. When our son was little, his play typically involved pushing toy trucks while making "power" noises. On the other hand, our daughter played house and family with dolls, all the while talking with them. When she was little she would often come into the bathroom where I was getting ready for the day, and, reaching over the counter top, she'd grab four bottles of whatever she could reach (such as a hairspray, deodorant, make-up, etc). Then she would dance them around saying, "Father, mother, sister, brother." She did this over and over! I didn't teach her that—it was wired into her as a girl to love family and relationships. And relationships thrive through communication.

This isn't to say that boys aren't communicators or that all girls like to chatter endlessly. But females are designed uniquely for nurturing bonds of intimate connection, and it operates through touch and speech. Speech is a gift from God to be used joyfully and appropriately. Women are meant to give the breath of life to another—to assist with encouragement, comfort, and words of wisdom, to lead with divinely inspired communication.

We see then, that a woman's design can be described as: a *completer, communicator,* and *promoter of life.* The numerical pictures of her nature are: *unity* (Aleph—1), *atonement* and *reconciliation* (Shin—300), and *grace* (Hey—5). The woman was made for unity and to also minister reconciliation in her territory, though her capacity in doing so was with the *dynamic of grace!* Her commission to rule and nature to bring reconciliation also made her a royal priestess. Yes, the man and woman were priests together!

Are you beginning to get a glimpse of your beautiful design as a woman? Do you see how God made male and female to interact harmoniously? Do you see how you, as a woman, are to release God's voice into your territory through grace?

UNITY OF THE GENDERS

From the beginning, male and female were the unified, yet individual, expression of *Elohim.* Together, their intimacy would be a beautiful dance of igniting and nurturing the purposes of God on earth.

In Hebrew, the two letters *Yod* and *Hey* actually combine to form the name of God—*Yah*! Did you hear that? Their unity would manifest His Name! Each one carried a unique part of Yah (or *Yaweh*), and when united they displayed His name. No wonder the enemy works so hard to create disunity.

God designed men and women to work together as His image to advance His Kingdom on earth. In the chapters ahead we will see how the Fall turned men and women's relationships upside-down, but also how Jesus reconciled all things back to God's original intent. The great manifestation of this grand reconciliation is our return to agreement with God. The second manifestation is the embrace of the sons and daughters in unity!

We are in the beginnings of a fresh move of God where many men are embracing the heart of God to lift women into the Father's full purposes of original intent. Likewise, a new company of women are rising to communicate what God is saying—no longer silent, and no longer speaking their own agenda, or Satan's!

The prophet Habakkuk foretold that God's glory would one day cover the earth (Hab. 2:14). This outpouring of glory signifies a restoration of unity; and unity creates an environment for divine blessing...and blessing promotes increase in every dimension. Jesus said that unity (not uniformity) is produced by the Father's glory (John 17:22).

It's time for an outpouring of God's glory!

It has taken a long time for some issues to be reconciled, but restored unity between believers, races, and the genders will be one of the marks of God's glory covering the earth in these last days.

As I expressed in the last chapter, because of the messaging I received through culture and religion, I felt unable to rise to destiny, and had a sense of being "less than" a male. But the Father showed me I am not, I am just wired a little different...a difference to be celebrated!

The Father is calling us to live confidently and synergistically, not timidly or competitively, but celebrating our authentic design.

The rich pages of God's Word begin with the picture of a man and his bride, and ends with a picture of Christ and His Bride. God is the greatest love-story Writer of all times, and His unfailing plan for all of us is the intimate union of our heart with His Son.

You may or may not have an earthly husband, but Jesus, the Ruler of the Nations, is the divine Husband who wants to launch you into the Father's full plan regarding you as His beloved daughter.

We've looked at our brilliant beginning, but there is more to see! We have only lifted the veil part way, so come with me as we continue bringing out treasures from the vault of truth about a woman's grand identity.

- 3 -

DANCES WITH SWORDS

"Woman is the full circle. Within her is the power to create, nurture, and transform."

— *Diane Mariechild*

A s women, most of us will admit that females are wired for the dramatic. Our very entrance started with drama — Adam on the surgery table and God pulling out a rib to make a woman. Yes, a little more dramatic than pottery making, if you ask me. Perhaps this is why we love gifts. After all, we started with a gift...a bone.

I'm sure that men today are thankful that chocolates and flowers will suffice over personal body parts. I also think we got the upgrade of designer material (bone versus dust). Maybe this plays into why grunge and sweat is a "manly" thing and why women like things to be more clean and neat. It's just a thought.

Before God fashioned the woman, He defined the aspects of Himself that would comprise her identity. Genesis 2:18 (Young's Literal Translation) says, "And Jehovah God saith, 'Not good for the man to be alone, I do make to him an *helper* as his *counterpart'"* (emphasis mine). Other translations say *suitable helper* or *helpmeet.*

Sometimes people say that a woman is a "helpmate" for the husband, but actually that isn't quite the term God used. A "mate" refers to a companion who accompanies or assists you, as an assistant to a more skilled worker. I love to be my husband's loving companion through life and assist him in anyway I can, because I love him. Love wants to help. However, God actually described His daughter as more than a *helpmate.* She has her own set of skills, too!

We are going to look now at that set of skills that God laced into the illustrious helper. Hold on to your hats—this term is filled with amazing details about a woman's identity!

THE INTUITIVE HELPER

What do you think of when you hear the word "helper"? Please allow me to give you a clue. It does NOT mean: maid, cook, or washwoman, even though we do these things because we like a clean home. There was more to the woman's creation than putting berries on the table and straightening a hammock, though this isn't to refute our displays of love for a husband.

The word *"helper"* (Heb. *"Ezer"*) means: *one who aids and assists to promote the progress or accomplishment of what is necessary to achieve an end.* God had a purpose in the earth that He wanted to accomplish, and *Ishshah* would have a grand part in promoting its progress toward fulfillment. While it would involve family and the home, it would also involve *all* of her gifts, including territorial dominion.

Most everywhere else in Scripture where *"Ezer"* is used, it refers to God Himself. It is the word that David used when asking God to be his Helper (Ps. 30:10; 54:4). This shows us that when God called her a "helper" it was no small thing! He defined her as one, who carrying His likeness, would bring *needed aid, strength, and skills for success.* She would bring heavenly assistance for what was lacking in accomplishing God's purposes on earth.

The Hebrew picture letters for *Ezer* are: Ayin, Zayin, and Resh.[1]

- *Ayin* means: eye, vision, insight
- *Zayin* is the picture of a weapon, meaning: to cut off
- *Resh* signifies: head or highest

These letters portrayed God's daughter as *a revelatory weapon for good who was of the highest order.* She was fashioned as a supreme class to bring the needed assistance for fulfilling divine intentions. Yes, this visionary leader would govern with the man.

Fashioned with a gift of *intuitive perception* she would see differently than him—from another perspective. As women, we all know how we can walk into a room and size things up. We look, perceive, feel the environment, check out what people are doing, what other women are wearing, and even make certain determinations about what's going on. Did you know this nature is actually a God-given gift (though sometimes skewed by our fallen nature)? We have been given an eye for assessing and discerning.

This visionary capacity is also called *intuition.* Women have special "antennas" in the places where they go and with the people they meet. They are sensitive as "seers," "feelers," and "knowers." They simply sense things, both positive and negative. This isn't to say that men are not, but women are more sensitive. This enhances their ability to aid and nurture as they evaluate needs.

Insight and revelation were special weapons given her to cut off the works of darkness. It was part of *Ishshah's* territorial watchmen calling. Hunches, feelings, and prophetic insight mix powerfully with the gift of communication for wisdom, counsel, prayer and intercession.

As we learned in the last chapter, men have an ability to wage war physically in defending territory, but women have a capacity of warring through awareness, assessment, and sensitivity by the Spirit.

The *helper* was given a special "eye" as part of her ability for being aware of things going on with her family, children, and territory, both naturally and spiritually. Let me give you an example: when a young mother is nursing, she looks into the eyes of her baby, forming a deep bond, as well as looking to make sure all is well. As mothers, we look at their little feet, hands, and body. We dress them and give our attention to making sure they are either warm or cool enough. We are always checking to see if they are well, no matter how old our children are.

When I was going through a very emotional time as a teen, I tried to run away three times. Each time, however, the Holy Spirit would tell my mother what I was up to and my endeavors were thwarted. I didn't like it, but I knew God was watching over me through my mother's intuitions. She was also a prayer warrior on my behalf. Thank God for praying mothers!

If you are praying for your child, don't give up! God hears the prayers of a mother. Pay attention to those feelings and insights, not in a paranoid way, but with wisdom from above.

WARRIOR BRIDE

This *Ezer* nature made the woman a *warrior bride*. She, after all, was like her Father who is a *Man of War* (Isa. 42:13). She was fashioned gentle, but not timid. She was equipped for peace and for war.

According to Hastings Dictionary of the Bible, the Hebrew wedding festivity in Judges 14 was portrayed in this way:

"The marriage festivity...is celebrated through eating, drinking, and merriment. Songs are sung during the festivity, in particular the praise of the bride's beauty while she, *in a sword dance,* displays the charms of her person by the flashing firelight. During the week, the pair are 'king and queen' enthroned on the threshing-board of the village."[2]

"She dances with swords and displays the charms of her person." That's right, no hiding, cowering, or cover-up—not kept in a backroom or silenced. I can see the couple now dancing together, bold and confident, by the fire light. Her flashing sword is the sword of truth, the Word of God. She handles it skillfully, like a Samurai with a two-edged blade. Her dance is the full and joyful expression of triumph and freedom. No victim mindset here!

It's okay to not be loud or extrovert; it is NOT okay to shrink back or be fearful...or even *falsely* humble.

I pray that the Holy Spirit is opening your eyes to see your own identity as a woman of spiritual vision and courage, sent by God, into this world. God did not make woman to be silent or passive, or with chains, *but as a warrior bride in assisting to cut off the enemy while progressing the purposes of God.*

The man and woman—the son and daughter—were sent here with a mission. The first revelation of God's likeness (the man) was apostolic; the second revelation of God's image (the woman) was the prophetic. Adam, male and female, was God's apostolic-prophetic team to govern the earth.

Now this isn't to say that only men can be apostles or women are prophets! Christ (the Great Apostle) distributes His gifts according to His choosing (as we will see more in a later chapter). What we do understand is that from the beginning, God established a foundation of male and female government, with apostolic and prophetic gifts, united to advance His Kingdom on earth as it is in heaven.

The numerical significance of *"Ezer"* portrays this bride as: *the sum and order of divine completion* (Ayin—70), *divine completion* (Zayin—7), and *the completed time of waiting with expectation* (Resh—200). Thus, *Ezer* signifies a *divine completion to what has been enduring in a state of waiting with expectation.*

Do you see how much of a "completing" nature woman carries? Adam was in a state of waiting for his counterpart who would assist him in completing the works of God. He couldn't do it alone. Then she, the helper, appeared. Again, completing a purpose is wired into our nature.

What an incredible portrait this intricate design is that also speaks of Christ who is waiting (with great expectation) for the completion of His own Bride. He is greatly anticipating His marriage supper with her...with us (Rev. 19:9). While we *are* complete in Him, we are also *being* completed in Him as the company of the Bride until the day He returns.

Each of us is still maturing individually in our life with Him, as well as maturing corporately. As the members of His Body we are learning to unite together as we co-labor with Him in completing the works of the Father. And too, the Body is being completed as more souls are born of God and made part of that great and radiant host of sanctified lovers.

Christ is looking with expectation for His Bride to emerge in the fullness of her identity in Him, to complete the works we are here to do. Jesus is waiting for His helper to join Him in bringing to fullness the purposes of the Father on earth—those good works that reconcile territories to the Father's love and design.

The earth too is waiting with expectation for the redeemed ones to rise and manifest the healing life of Christ (Rom. 8:19).

FACE-TO-FACE COUNTERPART

The other half of the term "help *meet*" means "*counterpart*" and is the Hebrew word *"Neged,"* which means: *what is in front of you, before your face, in front of your eyes, opposite you as one who corresponds to you.* A counterpart is: "one who holds a position or performs a function that corresponds to that of another person; an equivalent, peer, or equal."[3] Yes, a peer or equal!

The fish, fowl, and animals did not *correspond* as an equal to the man. But she did! She was his "kind": a *face-to-face* peer to help fulfill the purposes of God. She was not behind him, under his feet, or over his head. He wasn't dragging her by the hair and she wasn't yelling or trying to control him (at least not until after the Fall). She was his eye-to-eye co-worker and lover.

The Brown-Driver-Briggs Hebrew and English Lexicon says, "She corresponded to him as an equal and adequate to himself. This is confirmed in the meaning of what the man called her when he awoke *('bone of my bone and flesh of my flesh')*."[4]

The Hebrew picture letters for *counterpart* are: Nun, Gimmel, Dalet:

- *Nun* is represented by fish as: life, activity
- *Gimmel* is a camel meaning: to lift up
- *Dalet* again, is the picture of a door: passageway, path, entrance

These describe the woman as:

- One who promotes life, activity, and breakthrough
- One who uplifts and brings bountiful benefit
- One who is an access or gateway

In Hebrew, these portray her as *"The gate to life and wealth."* No wonder wise King Solomon said, "He who finds a wife finds a good (rich, valuable) thing and *obtains favor from the Lord"* (Prov. 18:22).

In ancient Mid-Eastern culture, camels spoke of wealth because of their ability to carry riches and goods across long stretches of desert terrain. Camels also lift and carry people. The woman was the man's peer, gifted with endurance, strength, and the ability to lift, encourage, and advance life.

This "lifting" ability is the likeness of God who lifts us from the deepest pits to stand on mountaintops with Him. Remember, the woman was fashioned to see beyond earth's limitations, receive revelation, and speak out hope and life to lift another into divine destiny.

The woman was given a divine ability to aid another's breakthrough into light-filled realms, giving her a regal position of being a *gateway to increase*. She had the capacity to carry goods, such as a child, across a long stretch of time until it reaches its destination—including an infant's time in the womb.

Do you see how much of a woman's design is linked to helping others in a beautiful realm of community? Even a simple warm smile, gentle touch, and the ability to encourage and comfort makes a difference in this world...let alone all the other treasured qualities a woman carries. Remember, all this is also a picture of Christ's Bride, too.

Ishshah was a gateway to increase whose abilities would prosper and advance life. God gave her as a blessing of Himself!

FASHIONED FOR COMMUNITY

The woman was designed for *relationship* and *community*. When it says that the *Yehovah Elohim* "fashioned" the rib into a woman, the word *"fashion"* (Heb. *"banah"*) means: to build, to fashion. It also means: *"behold a house of life!"* A house of life is a warm and **hospitable environment conducive to one's growth and increase**. A house is something that "surrounds" with **safety**, just like a rib does in protecting the heart and breath. A house is designed to be a loving place where people connect and relationships are nurtured.

Even her womb would be a surrounding, nurturing, protecting place. *Ishshah* carried *Elohim's* nature to advance the prosperity of family and intimate connection. She would make Adam feel loved, helped, connected and esteemed. She would be a safe place no matter what else was going on in his life. Her insights would lift his heart...no wonder he trusted her and why Satan would target her.

Just the fact that *Ishshah* was fashioned from his rib reflects her relational design. It spoke of how she would walk with him side-by-side, arm-in-arm. She wasn't taken from his head to tell him what to do, nor was she taken from his foot for him to walk on.

The surrounding nature in a woman is also seen in her protectiveness when it comes to children. A woman can move from sweet to fierce in a moment like a "mother bear." This is also an important part of God's image; He not only brings forth life, but He defends life and covers His family with His wings like a mother eagle (Ps. 91; Isa. 37:35).

Women have an ability to make others feel warm and welcomed. Hospitality is part of God's nature. A woman sets the timbre for the home with her words and actions, setting the tone in relationships by what she allows and doesn't allow. Even the way she cares for the home is an important part of relationship. Meal times are relationship-building times. A dinner is where Jesus performed His first miracle. The last thing we read in the Bible is about a dinner...the Lamb's supper.

One of the important dynamics of the early Church was the relational aspect of believers. Meeting in homes provided a hospitable environment for hearts to connect, lives to grow, gifts to operate, and the Spirit to move...and women had an important role in that, in every aspect! They were not silent observers as some may suppose.

Today, the importance of the home is often overlooked.

God loves family. Therefore, He blessed Adam, male and female, so that they would fill the earth with family...His family. Man was the catalyst and she the nurturer. Each had an important and needed part.

THE TIME KEEPER

One of my favorite aspects of *Ishshah* was the numerical significance for her as Adam's *counterpart* *("Neged"*: Nun, Gimmel, Dalet). It means: *celebration, jubilee, deliverance, and return to one's full inheritance* (Nun—50); *truth, reconciliation, and time* (Gimmel—3); and *the earth, its elements, and the name of God, thus the gateway between the seen and unseen world* (Dalet—4).

Ishshah's womanhood was laced with celebration, a jubilee…a party! She was a celebrated woman; there was NO shame or sorrow that she was female. Can you imagine *Ishshah* celebrating and bringing joy to *Iysh's* life? And she no doubt had all kinds of new ideas to implement in their tree-house abode.

She, like the man, was a gateway to unite the seen with the unseen, reconciling earth's elements with God's name, and more! God wove into the very fabric of her identity the promise of deliverance and a return to full inheritance—a promise not only for her, but that would impact the whole world. She may not have understood all these things at the time, but one day she would know the value of what she carried in divine promise. That promise would have a perfect timing for fulfillment, when all things would be reconciled to God in the Last Adam.

Timing is a part of the woman's design. We see it in myriad ways, including from the onset to conclusion of monthly cycles. Our bodies are regulated with synchronizations, including the precise interval that our body provides as a home for God to knit together a child within our womb. This applies to other things too that God gives us to "birth," whether in business, ministry, or other divine purpose.

So too, God's bride, Israel, is His divine clock in the earth. Watch major events with Israel—she is God's hour hand. The movements of His bridal timepiece also include His movement with His Church who is grafted into God's New Covenant with

Israel. These advancements are the ticking of Father's clock until the moment of Christ's return. As Christ's Bride, our life is to be in sync with His movement.

I want to pause here for just a moment and say that if you are reading this book and do not know Jesus, I warmly invite you to step into an encounter with Him. He loves you deeply and stands with arms open wide, longing to lift you into divine destiny with Himself. Talk to Him, He's listening.

AFFIRMED

Adam's first impression of the woman says volumes about his own perspective of her identity. *"This is now bone of my bones, and flesh of my flesh"* (Gen. 2:23a). He saw her as not just as his equal or kind, but as part of himself. She was not "lesser" than him, but was one with him. **His affirmation of their equality set the tone for their unity.**

You cannot have unity without equality. Too often the battle of the sexes has raged on the ground of mere equality, but God's design calls for something much higher: *unity*. So much in God is laced in the wonder of mystery that dynamics like unity can only be understood in part and through divine revelation of God's own relationship within Himself. We know in part now, but some day we will know in fullness. Nevertheless, we must grasp this truth of unity if we are to ever walk in the blessing and fullness of God's purposes.

Research shows that through the ages it has been assumed that the male's place is one of dominion over the woman, since he was formed first. But not only did such a picture NOT appear until after the Fall, but the important portrait Father was trying to paint in this whole beautiful creation sequence was, indeed, the opposite. He was painting a picture of the intimate unity, yet individuality, of those who comprised the likeness of His name. And Adam understood this when he said, "bone of my bone!"

69

This is how God made male and female. The woman, being fashioned from the protector, naturally looks for security...and not just security, but affirmation of who she is. We want to be seen and celebrated. Just as men, who are the preeminent *"Yod,"* look for honor...not in a prideful way, but they have a need to be respected and esteemed.

A few years ago, I conducted a women's survey. I asked what were some of the greatest needs they felt as a female. Bar none, they responded with "affirmation" as being either the top 1 or 2 on their list. Women around the world today are hungry to know their identity *and* feel affirmed in who they *are* as a woman ...not merely because of what they *do* for others.

I have learned, on a journey over many years, to not seek affirmation from a person, title, or position, because every one of these will fail me. I have learned to let God affirm me...and He gives it to me in loving abundance! Seeking it from another makes them a "god" in my life with standards set by ever changing human values. Nevertheless, this doesn't negate that God desires us to value and affirm one another; it's part of a culture of honor. I believe God especially wants the display of affirmation in marriage and family.

THE DYNAMIC DUO

God gave us a model for intimate human relationship through the first couple. Marriage is more than a license and living together, it is a covenant of love, honor, and unity in life purpose. How utterly different this is from the picture I was shown as a young person of a man being a "hammer" over a wife...and in the name of Christianity!

"For this reason shall a man leave his father and mother
and cleave unto his wife" (Gen. 2:24).

When the Father presented His daughter, it was, as we read a moment ago, "a good thing." It was a divine gift to shower him with needed help. In receiving this gift, she *belonged* to him—not as a possession to do with as he wanted, but as his own body to be cherished, nurtured, and cared for so that together, they would come into a fruitful destiny in the purposes of God.

This belonging was also two-way! As the great love-writer, Solomon, put it: "I am my beloved's and he is mine" (Song of Sol. 6:3).

In this face-to-face unity, the man and woman were heaven's government on earth as:

- Apostle and Prophet
- Hand and Helper
- Power and Revelator
- Worker and Promoter
- Spark and Breath
- Catalyst and Completer
- Divine Order and Divine Grace
- Priest and Priestess

Do you see the beautiful and synergetic dance that happens when the gifts unite?

When men and women unite in Christ in a culture of love and honor we will have a force yet unseen! We will see heaven on earth. We will see the name of God manifested...it's what the earth is groaning to see (Rom. 8:19).

Our brilliant beginning was the fiery revelation of both sonship and brideship. We need the revelation of both—of who we are as sons and daughters to our Father, and our identity as a Bride to Christ. The world began with the story of a marriage and it will culminate in a marriage—the marriage supper of the Lamb.

The woman was an integral part of God's plan from the beginning, the final touch to creation's story. She was the grand finale to a brilliant symphony of sound that became matter, and from the matter a man was formed, and from his bone was made a woman. Together they walked as the united flame of God's name on earth.

It is time for us to cast off the shackles of false identities. It's time to be those intuitive weapons and face-to-face helpers, whether single or married, but certainly as a fiery Bride for the Son...a Bride who dances with a sword.

- 4 -

FATAL ATTRACTION

*"Remember, no one can make you feel inferior
without your consent."*

— Eleanor Roosevelt

We were fashioned by Divine Love—to love and be loved. Nevertheless, love has its challenges, adversities, and strong adversaries.

We have an especially potent adversary named Satan, whose name is also *Abbadon*—the father of destruction. We must not be ignorant of his schemes. I will use this name, *Abbadon*, when referring to Satan, because it so well fits who he is and what he does on earth…he destroys.

I have learned that to overcome in life and live in the fullness of my Father's glorious plans, I must know three critical elements:

1. Know God
2. Know who I am
3. Understand my enemy

Every great general and warrior will tell you this same truth. God put the man and woman in a specific place with dominion for its wellbeing. They had dominion not just to trim hedges and mend broken bird wings, but authority over any opponent who would enter and bring harm to the land beneath their rule. They were to reconcile everything to the designs of God.

We've unveiled the beauty of how God has wired both men and women, now let's look at how *Abbadon* is "wired" as he plots against our success in life, and in God. We have a battle to win and we can't be ignorant. Let's look at how life unfolded for the woman in the garden and the enemy's method of operation against her. His tactics never change.

THE TRICKSTER

Into the garden there crept another life form, one of God's exquisite creations, but who had fallen from his original state. He had been the anointed Cherub assigned to cover God's throne. His very being was designed with music and frequencies whenever he moved. His garments had been made of precious gems and the place of glory fire had been his home. Pride, however, had moved him to betray God and seek a throne for himself, above God's. Having spurred a great rebellion, war ensued in the heavens that ended with his expulsion...and a third of the angels trailing behind him.

Now, an outcast from the celestial realm, his power lay in his ability to deceive. He became a dark shadow that emulates "light," but is not. This creation turned out to be an evil adversary, a cunning foe, and a malevolent despiser of *Elohim* and all that concerns Him. This creature's name was Lucifer, also known as Satan, Destroyer, Ruler of darkness, Accuser, Murderer, Tempter, Thief, (among other names), and, of course, *Abbadon*.

Denied his proud and illegal claim to heaven's throne, he pursued a new venue: earth's throne. Only this time, he didn't have to depose God himself, just God's son and daughter...the newlyweds.

The enemy assessed his targets. He would not fail this time. He analyzed the two as they strolled, arm in arm, among the lush flora.

"Unity," he mumbled, "it will not last if I can help it...and I will!"

He saw that she had a heightened gift of revelation...this allured his ego. He surmised that deception would be an excellent weapon of choice: manipulate her thoughts, incite hostile feelings toward God, and seduce her with lies...after all, it worked with a third of the angels. He would make her feel betrayed by the Maker and incomplete in who she was. He would alter her focus. He would disable this delicate but powerful *weapon of God* with trickery. He would destroy the *house* that God built.

Now, what about the man? Hmm, if she were won over, it would force the man to choose alliance between Father and his "other half." It was a fifty-fifty chance...but betting on her power of influence and the man's desire for her, it just might work. If the plan succeeded, the man would blame her. Resent her. It would tear their relationship apart.

Perfect.

Like a master magician, the dark angel formulated an illusion that would prompt her engagement with his evil counsel, while the real trick ensued: steal earth's throne.

Seeking out the perfect cloak, he chose the form of a serpent and made his approach to *Ishshah*...his scheme well planned out.

Tactic #1: Create mistrust—twist God's words, cause confusion, discombobulate her thinking:

"Did God really say you must not eat the fruit from *any* of the trees in the garden?" [1]

"Oh no!" she replied. "We can eat from every tree except the one right in the middle of the garden—we can't even touch it lest we die!"[2]

Perfect! The mere presence of the liar was already having its effect as she blurted out an exaggeration of what God said. Now, deepen that mistrust by accusing the Father of lying and having ill intentions toward her. Slander His character!

"You won't die!" the serpent hissed. "God knows that your eyes will be opened and you'll be just like Him, knowing both good and evil."[3]

Tactic #2: Showcase the deadly fruit—shift the focus of her eyes. Lure her with what will *enhance* her insight.

"She *saw* that the tree was beautiful and its fruit *looked* delicious, and she wanted the *wisdom* it would give her. So she took some of the fruit and ate it."[4]

Tactic #3: Sit back and let the communicator share her experience—the man won't want to be left out or feel "lesser than."

"Then she gave some to her husband, who was with her, and he ate it, too."[5]

And in a moment's time it was done. Over. It played out simply and quickly. Like a snake striking its victim. What the serpent didn't expect was the ease in which it all happened. No fight. No struggle. Not even an argument or defense of the Creator. Not from her or the man, the keeper of the garden…who knew exactly what he was doing. There he stood. Passive. Not saying a word. Juice dripping down his chin.

"A rebel just like me," mocked the serpent.

And the world changed.

Adam broke covenant with God and the light within the rulers' spirit went dark.

THE COURTROOM

God came to the garden where the two were. And instead of receiving Him with their usual warm welcome they were now hiding, trying to figure out how to cover their nakedness with leaves. God called for the man whom He had specifically given command to guard the garden. Timidly coming from behind a bush, the man admitted his fear and blamed the woman who blamed the serpent who devised the fall of the house that God built.

Choices.

The man, the woman, and the serpent were summoned to the Judge's tribunal table.

Two trembled. One sneered. All were guilty.

The gavel of consequence struck.

God to the serpent: "You are cursed. You will crawl on your belly and eat dust. Perpetual enmity will be between your seed and the woman's seed, but her seed will crush your head, and you will bruise his heel."[6]

God to the woman: "You will have sorrow in bringing forth children; you will desire your husband and he will rule over you."[7]

God to the man about the ground: "The ground is now cursed..."

God to the man about himself: "...Your work will be filled with sorrow as the earth will be against you, growing thistles and thorns; and you will return to the dust from which you were made."[8]

The judgment invoked, the serpent slithered away, seizing the now vacated throne as "god of this world."

"How utterly simple," he laughed. "How effortlessly they bow to me."

Life choices reflect the voice we embrace and the One we reject.

THE OUTCASTS

The fallen cherub had triumphed. The whole earth shuddered beneath the thunderous clamp of his yoke. The curse spread quickly like a crawling vine. The dark hosts who accompanied *Abbadon* celebrated over the new race of fallen creatures: mankind. Earth was now theirs to rule with Adam's seed under their dominion.

This new government affected everything. Even the creatures that had run freely to the children of Light now scattered in fear from them as the couple donned the draping of slain animal skin...a sacrifice God made to cover their nakedness. Death was the display of sin's penalty.

Nevertheless, it was also a prophetic promise of a day coming where another would be slain for man's sin—a Lamb whose sacrifice would crush the head of the serpent and free mankind from the law of sin and death. God in flesh would become the sinless offering to redeem man back to Himself by way of a New Covenant.

But for now, Adam, like the fallen creation before him, was cast out of God's presence and driven from his assigned place. Now they would wander. Fallen begets fallen.

ISHSHAH GETS A NEW NAME

Ishshah stood there, ashamed and blamed, feeling the unbearable weight of having been a misguided weapon and promoter of false insight...a failed leader. How would she be trusted now? Rather

78

than advance Father's purposes, she had partnered with His enemy to thwart them. If only she hadn't listened to the serpent.

When I began to study this passage, it was the first action that Adam took following the divine pronouncement that shook me — he named her.

"Now the man called his wife's name Eve, because she was

the mother of all the living" (Gen. 3:20).

It sounds right, after all, she was designed to be a mother! Prior to this, however, it was the animals under *their* rule that he named; now she was under his rule. They were no longer *as one.* They were no longer "Adam" together—he was Adam and she was Eve. Having lost his authority at the Fall, she was the one thing that he, the powerful *Yod*, had to govern. It was logical that his first bill to pass in his new (demoted) office would be to name what he ruled...her.

The Hebrew picture letters for *Eve* ("*Chavvah*") are:

- *Chet*, a private chamber, fence, inner room
- *Vav*, a nail, add, secure
- *Hey*, window, behold, reveal

Her new name spoke of her capacity as a mother to provide a private chamber for a human baby to form and develop, for those "inward parts" to be knit together with life. She too had lost authority at the Fall, but she was still the protector and promoter of human life.

Ishshah lost unity with *Iysh*, but in this she could be fruitful in Father's purpose to fill the earth. It was a gift of the highest order. What a glory. What a privilege! It was a grand affirmation of magnificent design. Nevertheless, somehow the naming carried with it somberness. While honored to be given the name of *mother*, she knew that somehow her identity had been redefined. She was no longer his face-to-face counterpart. He no longer called her *Ishshah* as one with himself, *Iysh*. She had become "less than."

Nevertheless, she also had a promise from Father — her seed would crush the head of the one who had deceived her. And somewhere hidden in the depth of her soul was still imprinted *"Neged"* — a divine restoration to full inheritance that would one day come.

The name "Eve" represented a beautiful, though limited, function under a new world order. Had her name change come before the Fall, I wouldn't think it so significant. But somehow the words of her fallen husband, while true, carried an identifying decree of what she would now do, rather than who she was in unity with him.

She had experienced a realm of glory from the beginning. She had been created as the daughter of the great I AM to experience dominion alongside the man. Now, a cloud darkened her identity as one confined to a position under his rule.

How would she now walk out this terrible death sentence? Not only was there a spiritual abysm between her and the Creator, but a deep chasm in her relationship with her husband.

A FALLEN DOMINION

While the blessing of God creates a rich supply that empowers life and prosperity; a curse is what causes withering, lack, and chaos. At the Fall, the word of judgment that he would *"rule"* over her, was not the same as the word "rule" in Genesis 1:28 where both were given dominion.

The word *"rule"* in Genesis 3:16 is *"mashal"*: Mem (overpower, chaos) and *Shin* (consume, overcome) and *Lamed* (to goad, control, authority). This type of rule literally means: "The chaos that consumes through control." It means: to rule, reign, have dominion, *control,* to order with authority, give sentence, lord over, and in the worst sense: **tyranny**.

Adam's rule as "lord over" his wife was never God's original design.

80

Proverbs 29:2 uses this same word *"mashal"* as a sad portrayal of what happens when a wicked man *rules*: "When the righteous increase, the people rejoice; but when a wicked man rules [mashal], the people groan" (clarification mine).

To be clear, ruling over her was NOT a command that God gave to the man; it was the judgment that God told the woman would RESULT from their actions of eating from the tree of the knowledge of good and evil. *It was a result of spiritual death.*

The rule that God gave to both the man and woman at creation was *"Radah"* (*Resh*—head; *Dalet*—door; and *Hey*—window). It means: dominion, reign over, subjugate, chastise, tread as a wine press. It was not a rule of chaos, rather of keeping creation in submission to divine authority. And this, by the way, was exactly what they DIDN'T do in the garden. They didn't keep creation (namely, the serpent) in subjection, chastised, and under righteous rule. Rather, it was allowed to lie, slander the Creator, and incite rebellion against Him.

Dominion was given to both male and female regarding the earth. Original design did NOT give dominion to the man over the woman. Together they were God's governors to ensure the peace of their territory. Peace in Hebrew ("Shalom") means more than just tranquility, it means: "the authority that destroys chaos."

Precious woman, everything that I am speaking about is to show you the truth about God's original design with us as His daughters. We were fashioned to rule with authority, together with men, in the purposes of our Heavenly Father. Subjugation was never our place until the Fall, from which we have been completely redeemed through Christ (which we will look at shortly). But for now, I am showing you clearly the demise that happened when we all fell for Satan's deception and ate from the tree of the knowledge of good and evil.

Understanding history empowers us to know God's will and the enemy's schemes. God wants us to get back into our proper identity with Him through Christ, for the effective work He has appointed for us as His daughters.

THE DESIRE-RULE PARADIGM

The word *"desire"* (Heb. *"tĕshuwqah"*) means: longing, desiring, craving, stretching out after as man to woman, woman to man, or even as a beast to devour a prey. Because we came from man, it is natural for us to desire a man in our life. However, at the Fall, a "desire" was released that would keep her stretching out after him, no matter what his rule looked like, and a "stretching out after" that would even seek control over him.

This *devouring* is also portrayed in Proverbs as the seductive woman, and also a quarrelsome woman—one who shames the husband, is ill-tempered, or unfaithful.[9] In other words, her desire would be just as chaotic as his newly found rule.

I'm sure many of us have our stories of how we have "stretched out after" a man in wrong ways. We have either allowed someone to control or dominate us, or we have tried to control another through our own manipulative words, erratic emotions, or self-centered actions. We have done things our own way, instead of God's way.

The two words, *desire* and *rule* (which I will now term as the *desire-rule* paradigm), that were pronounced on the woman have become the two greatest factors to impact all women, in all generations, and in all cultures including religious cultures, from then until now. We must see this origin and know that today we have deliverance and a restored paradigm in Christ.

The questions for the first couple then were: would Adam rule with kindness or sink into tyranny? Would he protect and prosper the woman or abuse and control her? And how would Eve respond to him? Would she desire him so much that she would be a *doormat* (silent submission to unrighteous control)? Or would she try to control and dominate him (be a *devourer*)?

82

The Fall was a complete paradigm shift for male and female, as well as for the entire world that had been assigned to their care. The pronouncement was not God's desire, but a consequence of spiritual death induced by the source they ate from.

Wrong choices can throw us into places we never imagined. Places we never wanted to be. Places that redefine us, and even rename us, giving us an altered identity. Yet even in our worst state, God has only one definition of us: loved and valued. And for that reason, He works ceaselessly and untiringly to let us know that we are His desire. His answer to our every dilemma is always divine provision because of His unending love for us.

THE PROMISE AND THE ENMITY

The Fall not only created a chasm in man's relationship with God, but a ruin in mankind's associations with one another. It turned everything upside down. Inverted. Altered. Twisted.

I find it interesting that the first thing the man and woman did was to try to cover their nakedness, that being, their *gender differences*. Before the Fall, under the glory of God's presence that covered them, gender differences weren't noticed. Gender wasn't an "issue" until they turned from God.

Since then, there has been a discord in gender relationships that has perversely played out through history...often on catastrophic levels. It is not a victim statement to say that women have been impacted in a way somewhat different than men. It's just a fact, though the whole world has suffered from the choices made that day in the garden.

Satan started a war, nevertheless, God declared the victory. And guess who He chose as His vessel to usher in the appearance of the Triumphant One and Redeemer of mankind?

A woman!

However, such privilege would not be without cost.

"I will put enmity [hostility] between you and the woman, between your seed and her seed, and He will strike [crush] your head and you will strike [bruise] his heel" (Gen. 3:15).

God established enmity between the serpent and the woman, between his seed and hers, with the intent to bring vindication of His own name. We know the story of how Jesus, the promised Seed born of a virgin, was bruised for our iniquity as He crushed Satan's dominion on the cross.

Because of redemption, every child born into this world adds to the earth another life filled with divine potential. Every human heart is an impending weapon in Christ's hand to be filled with divine light in destroying the works of darkness. Every life is a prospective arrow to be placed in Father's quiver against the encroachment of hell on earth—a holy fire to continue defeating Satan's dominion. No wonder there is such hostility towards women *and* unborn babies!

The seed from the fruit of the tree of the knowledge of good and evil continues to permeate the souls of mankind today. We know it as the sin nature. It carries the serpent's voice that whispers as wisdom from below, rather than from above. In fact, the Hebrew word for snake (*nachash*) is "the moving whisper" and "sin" (Heb. *chatah*): the fence of the snake's strength.

In the next chapter we are going to look at how the snake continued to coil itself around male-female relationships. We will see how customs emerged built on the judgment of the desire-rule paradigm, forging chains around the woman. We will also see later how some of these customs have prevailed in Christian culture, and not just in male-female relationships, but in the Church's own identity as a Bride!

This is an important understanding not just for us, but for the whole Church to see where we've relentlessly held high the desire-rule paradigm, even above redemption. Not only has it kept women in chains, but in doing so it has disempowered Christ's Body—**a Bride often seen toiling *for* God in a powerless** judgment culture, rather than living with authority as a full co-laborer with Christ. Such is the mark of an altered-design.

Come with me now as I unveil the past to aid you in stepping confidently into a present and future with power.

- 5 -

THE WOMAN'S JOURNEY

*"Let us not seek to fix the blame for the past. Let us accept
our own responsibility for the future."*

– John F. Kennedy

Through the centuries, men and women have embraced, fought, supported, suppressed, and often related to one another in a muddled mixture of love and control. Both have found deep satisfaction in each other's arms, and both have suffered from the onslaught of brutal words and unkind actions hurled at them from the opposite sex.

While they have each had their own journey of struggles, the woman's has been a bit different. In the next few pages, we are going to look at "Eve's" journey (referring to women in general) that ensued from the garden. Understanding some basic historical events will help you see how mindsets about women formed in a fallen world, and how customs and traditions developed in cultures regarding the helper's role. However, as we read, we must also remember the divine promise of victory ahead for her.

As we see the woman's journey unfold and her status decline, be mindful that this is not simply about men versus women, but is a *spiritual warfare* being played out on many fronts, including gender issues. It is part of Satan's enmity regarding the woman...regarding God's image in both genders.

We've seen how God sent the woman as an incredible face-to-face helper, but how the Fall with an altered paradigm changed everything. The earth, now under the rule of *Abbadon's* hand, was watered by the acid rain of his hatred.

The *Yod's* nature became corrupt, and rather than embracing the helper, his hand now suppressed her. He had trusted her insight, but had been betrayed. Deeply. She was no longer his face-to-face counterpart. He no longer affirmed her. Her dance with swords was replaced by the ball and chain of a lesser and redefined identity.

Without the flame of the Spirit to purify and energize motives, his nature to order things became laced with ego. Her own gift of vision was dark, and unable to see the heavenly realm, she looked to the man for protection in any way she could. Her gift of words turned to silence, though often finding her voice in a seducing or daggering display.

It is *Abbadon's* nature to destroy. His sole purpose is to steal, kill, and bring to ruin by inspiring chaos, and most specifically in relationships. While we look at human events, I pray that we read with eyes of the Spirit, holding tight to the grace that is to be revealed.

"EVE" IN ANCIENT CULTURES

In most ancient cultures, the desire-rule paradigm incurred an immense loss of identity for women, "*as childbearing became almost her sole purpose in society.*" These are not my own thoughts, but extensive research has confirmed this line of thinking. Though the woman's place became increasingly harsh, children were needed as the survival of a society, and "Eve" was important in this role.

As ancient cultures evolved, there were varying levels of women's social status. In Sumerian society, men and women were on a near equal status. Though society was patriarchal, women were still seen as influential. Their standing was high as they held an active role in both the economy and court. They were businesswomen, physicians, performers, artists, and writers. Women participated as scribes, priestesses, owned real estate, as well as being vested in inheritances right along with males.

Since female goddesses held importance in their religious worship, it helped give women a respected role in society. That is, until the second millennium when gods reflected a society in which men became predominant.[1]

In ancient Egypt (approx. 1400 B.C.), women were still enjoying some parity with men and, theoretically, with equal legal and economic rights. They could manage, own, and sell private property including slaves, land, portable goods, servants, livestock, and money. Women could sue, marry, divorce, free slaves and make adoptions. Wives kept their independence and controlled their own assets.[2]

With time, however, the decline of gender relationships in most cultures intensified. The status of women varied from one civilization to another, but in many cultures her role became grim. There were some (though few), who dared to supersede the growing barriers as limitations in their ability to prosper alongside men deepened.

"Still viewed as an important component to continuing a society's survival, her conditions, nevertheless, were often harsh and her status was often nearly appalling. Work for women became largely limited to being household servants, and gender bias played a strong hindrance in the ability of single women to support themselves."[3] This augmented her need for a man's protection and provision.

89

Research shows the continued downturn of how women were viewed. Though she was seen as a "creative source of human life, historically women have been considered not only intellectually inferior to men, but also a major source of temptation and evil." As Greek mythology later put it, she was "Pandora who opened the forbidden box and brought plagues and unhappiness to mankind."[4]

Such views were nothing less than *Abbadon* fanning the flame of bitter blame against the helper.

WRITTEN CODES FOR WOMEN

It's one thing to have a concept about another person, but something happens when that idea goes to print. And no matter whether the words are right or wrong, the very fact that it's written gives it a new authority as "truth"...even if it's not.

In approximately 2050 B.C., the *Code of Ur-Nammu* was written in the Sumerian language, a culture in which women had, until then, enjoyed many freedoms. This law system was the oldest written *societal law code* that introduced a new cultural demonstration of a harsher treatment of women.

A few centuries later, in approximately 1686 B.C., the *Code of Hammurabi* (King of Babylon of ancient Iraq) was produced in the Akkadian language. This code became the first set of ancient laws *written for all citizens to read*. Its purpose was to bring order and justice to Babylonian society. Its laws were supposed to protect the poor and weak. However, many of its laws reflected strong gender bias as family laws were often about controlling women. Hammurabi felt to write these laws to please his gods (namely the Sun god, Shamash), of whom he declared himself to be a chosen favorite. By writing the 252 laws on stone, they were considered "untouchable" (hence the term "written in stone").[5]

Some laws protected women, recognizing their need for legal protection from male authority. However, under these laws, women were often treated as children, even noted as nothing more than chattel or slaves. **"The written Code of Hammurabi introduced new restrictions on women that hadn't been in effect before, reducing a wife's role to that of a maid-servant and the idea of her as being subservient to her husband was established."** 6

"These new written laws gave power of husbands over their wives, but also to the fathers as well. In fact, a woman never really left the control of her father who retained strict control over his daughters even when married. Marriage, celibacy, the right to bear children, being given as service to the gods or being sold were all at the discretion of the father. The Hammurabi law system left little room for a woman's rights. Hammurabi's Code has stood as the symbol for written law for thousands of years."7

The law stated that if the woman was a "bad wife," her husband had options including:

1. Send her away and keep the children and dowry

2. Make her a slave in her own household

A woman could file suit if her husband treated her cruelly or neglected her, however, she could only get a judicial separation and there was no judgment or punishment for his behavior towards her. If she proved her case, she might walk away with her dowry, but if she did not prove her case she could be drowned.

Other laws didn't just punish women, but instead put them in inferior positions of obedience and second-class citizenship. A man couldn't sleep with another man's wives, slaves, or single women, but he was free to exploit any woman under his own service.8

GOD'S WRITTEN CODE

As civilizations grew and the treatment of women continued to decline, God called out a people to Himself to be a beacon of light in the midst of the nations—Israel. And to this people, He gave His own "written code" called the Torah. With His own divine finger He wrote of the equal importance of honoring a father and a mother (Exod. 20:12). Under Moses' leadership, God raised up a standard in the earth to make His name and glory known, and to instruct His people in how they were to treat Him and one another. The Holy Spirit inspired Moses in writing the Torah, the books of Moses (Genesis through Deuteronomy), which included the Ten Commandments and 613 commands (Mitzvot). These divine laws were distinguished from every other legal code in the ancient Near East. Offences were recognized not merely as being against another person or society as a whole, but against God.

In God's written code, love and honor was established as the basis of connection with Him and others. A woman wasn't simply viewed for bearing children, but was seen as the one who inspires the entire tone of the home and thus its influence in society. Though women's responsibilities were different than men's, they were no less important. While her place was mostly in the home, she was encouraged to prosper in her own business (Prov. 31). Women were honored in leadership such as with Miriam and Deborah, a judge in Israel. A woman's spiritual gifts were embraced such as with Huldah the prophetess, and others. In fact, seven of the fifty-five prophets were women. "Respect was accorded to women as a part of Jewish ethnic culture."[9]

Even when Sarah called Abraham "lord" (Adon), it was not as we think in terms of control and subjection. It was a beloved term of honor used as an expression of love for the man's protection, provision and goodness toward her. Abraham was the master of his household, but treated Sarah like a princess! God also told Abraham, "Listen to your wife!" (Gen. 18:12; 21:12)

Though women were not encouraged to pursue higher education or religious pursuits, it was primarily because of the honored importance of their responsibility as wives and mothers. Women were able to hold titles of position. The rights of women in ancient Israel were greater than what women in America had known until the 20th century. They could buy, sell, own property, and make their own contracts. In fact, Proverbs 31 is traditionally read at Jewish weddings as it speaks repeatedly of business intelligence as a trait to be prized in women. Proverbs 31 is also the *blessing* that a husband speaks over his wife every week on Shabbat!

It's said that women "had the right to be consulted with regard to their marriage. Marital sex was regarded as the woman's right, and not the man's. Men did not have the right to beat or mistreat their wives, a right that was not recognized by law in many Western countries until recent times. In cases of rape, a woman was generally presumed *not* to have consented to the intercourse, even if she enjoyed it, even if she consented after the sexual act began and declined a rescue...Traditional Judaism recognized that forced sexual relations even within the context of marriage [were] rape and [were] not permitted."[10]

In ancient Hebrew culture, children were to revere *both father and mother*. While Exodus 20:12 notes the father first, in Leviticus 19:3 it notes the mother first, intentionally showing that both parents are equally entitled to honor and respect. King Solomon wrote this to his royal sons: "Listen to your father's instruction and do not forsake your mother's teaching" (Prov. 1:8). In fact, the whole book of Proverbs is devoted to paying attention to wisdom's voice portrayed by what? Yes, a woman!

Though a woman also portrays the seducer's voice too, it doesn't lessen the first picture. **What it does reflect is the power of a woman's influence in what she communicates — through words *and* actions.**

Even though traditional Judaism, from then until now, has held a woman's role to be primarily as a wife, mother and keeper of the home, Judaism has had great respect for the importance of her role and her spiritual influence over her family. In ancient scriptures where the reigns of Israel's kings are recorded, the mother's name is mentioned repeatedly in link with a royal son who ascended to the throne. Such mention denotes her influence...whether for good or bad!

Because the Jewish religious life revolved around the home, and not the synagogue (unlike traditional Christianity where religious life is often centered in church activities), the woman's role there was every bit as important as the man's. She was exempted from the duty of prayer times not because she wasn't allowed by her gender, but because her presence and duties in the home were so important. As one resource puts it:

> "After all, a woman couldn't be expected to just drop a crying baby when the time comes to perform a mitzvah. She couldn't leave dinner unattended on the stove while she attended an evening prayer service. It is this exemption from certain religious activities that has led to the greatest misunderstanding of the role of women not only in Judaism, but in traditional Christianity as well. Some mistake this exemption as a prohibition. However, not being required does not mean they were not permitted to observe prayer and roles in religious gatherings. However, because of the exemption, some perceive that women have no role in Jewish (or Christian) religious life. But it is a misconception. In Judaism (also unlike traditional Christianity), God was not viewed as exclusively male or masculine but that God has both masculine and feminine qualities. To think of Him as male or female was absurd. They understood that 'man' was created with dual gender and was later separated into male and female."[11]

Not only did God support the dignity of women in His "code," He called Israel as His own beloved Bride. He called Himself a Husbandman to Israel and demonstrated before the nations what the role of a Husband is in tender love, care, protection, and provision (Isa. 54:4). He empowered His Bride to prosper in every way. God still stands as Israel's Husbandman and Protector today.

God's written and living code of love regarding men and women was demonstrated clearly through Israel's ancient culture. Many of the laws regarding women in pagan cultures were NOT a reflection of God's heart. They were a reflection of an upside down world living apart from authentic design.

FROM DIVINE POLICY TO FOREIGN CAPTIVITY

Israel, however, did not keep her heart in the love of God. In spite of His continual beckoning to her to remain faithful in covenant, she continually ran after the gods of other nations. Divine protection was ultimately removed, and in approximately 732 B.C., Israel was taken into captivity by Assyria. Judah soon followed in Israel's footsteps and in approximately 597 B.C., she was taken captive under Babylonian rule for 70 years.

During that time of captivity, two major events occurred that have greatly impacted women, even to today:

- Compulsory use of *the veil*
- The commenced writing of the *Babylonian Talmud*

THE VEILING BEGINS

Assyrian law code was notable for its brutal and repressive attitude towards women, making her status even less favorable than under the Code of Hammurabi. Women were considered no more than chattel, and by now Assyrian law dictated that all women (except harlots) were to wear a veil in public. Neither wives, daughters of lords, widows or Assyrian women were to go out on the street without having their heads covered—whether with a shawl, robe or mantle.[12] In fact, prostitutes and slave women were forbidden to wear a veil, and could be punished for doing so.[13]

The veil served as "a way of protecting a father or husband's interest in his daughter or wife. The face of a married or

95

marriageable woman could not tempt or 'allure' men from beneath a veil. Wives, daughters, and widows would be severely punished for not covering their faces in public. But punishments also extended to male observers. If a man recognized a prostitute or slave woman wearing a veil and did not report her to an authority, he could be publicly flogged (beaten), mutilated (having his hand chopped off, for example), or imprisoned."[14]

Veiling became a cultural norm as a sign of chastity – though that chastity was more about protecting the man's mind than her conduct!

As the Assyrian Empire transitioned to Persian rule under Cyrus (5th century B.C.), the veil was used more as a sign of the delineation between the elite class and common women.

Veiling was a common use in the Persian Empire, though it was somewhat different in Greece (that was just beginning its ascent to world influence). There, women were veiled in a variety of forms, though not necessarily as compulsory, and neither did the absence of a head covering imply the woman to be immoral (as in Assyrian culture[15]). In fact, regarding religious practices, "there are clear indications that it was custom for women to take part in rituals with their heads uncovered, such as with the cult of the goddess Demeter, or in the worship of Dionysus, where the female celebrants known as 'maenads' not only came with uncovered heads, but also let down their hair and danced in public processions. Priestesses most probably presented offerings without head-coverings."[16]

This is important in light of 1 Corinthians 11 where the controversy about veiling occurs (which we will look at later). Since veiling wasn't based on God's laws but on pagan culture, Paul's ultimate word in addressing this issue was: "we have no such custom." The letter he wrote to the Church at Corinth was not a stamp of affirmation on this custom, but an explanation of the argument that was taking place there. As we will see, Paul's missionary journey's and letters were full of admonitions about what the gospel is really about, and a counter to the many philosophies formed in pagan cultures and Talmud customs (as you will now see).

FORGING THE CHAINS OF TRADITION

Prior to captivity, women in Hebrew culture fared much better under God's laws. However, during the time of captivity, as mentioned, a new code was written by Jewish spiritual leaders that was not God's code. This is where, dear ones, we will now put on our "forgiveness glasses" as we glimpse yet another written set of practices.

During Babylon captivity Jewish rabbis began compiling a set of laws called the *Babylonian Talmud*. This rabbinical literature was a compilation of oral laws, customs and teachings from numerous rabbis and covered various topics on law, history, and lore, including views of women. This Talmud is the basis for all codes of rabbinic law and was esteemed, by them, as only second to the Torah (the Law of Moses). While God had given Moses His laws that protected women and esteemed mothers, these oral traditions of men were not always so "women friendly," and often reflected the influence of the Assyrian culture in which they lived. It was the oral laws and man-made traditions that Jesus (and later Paul) opposed in dealing with Israel's spiritual leaders, specifically the Pharisees.

Ah yes, the ideas we think of in times of bondage. I don't know whether the rabbis just didn't have anything better to do while being away from their land (and their temple destroyed) or what. Perhaps feeling "bullied" by captors made them want to bully someone else. In this case, being immersed in a culture that was terribly, often brutally, unfavorable toward women, perhaps made women an easy target.

A note to remember: a religious idea isn't necessarily God's idea. As followers of Truth, we must be careful of what mindsets from culture we are adopting as our "norm" that are not God's "norms" for us—ways that are not heaven's culture.

Here are just a few of the Talmud traditions regarding the female gender:[17]

- *"A woman's voice is prohibited because it is sexually provocative" (Talmud, Berachot 24a).*
- *"Women are sexually seductive, mentally inferior, socially embarrassing, and spiritually separated from the law of Moses; therefore, let them be silent" (summary of Talmudic sayings concerning women).*
- *"It is a* **shame** *for a woman to let her voice be heard among men" (Talmud, Tractate Kiddushin).*
- *"The voice of a woman is filthy nakedness" (Talmud, Berachot Kiddushin).*

Instructors of the law even used scripture to support some of these views, such as in the Midrash (rabbinical literature) where the Hebrew interpretation of Psalms 45:14 is: *kol kevuda bat melekh penima*: "all the princesses' treasure is stored within."

This was used as authority for *female domesticity*—"stored within" meaning an enforced staying at home. One resource explains it this way:

> "Some rabbis simply have seen discrimination against women as being necessary for the functioning of society. Women are worse off than men, but there is simply no practical way to root-out the causes of women's oppression without overthrowing the very foundations of human society."[18]

Also in the rabbinical literature was a list from oral tradition called the *"Ten Curses of Eve."*[19] This was an expansion of the curse pronounced on the woman in the garden and explained that "'He shall rule over thee,' as the wife being in total submission and subjugation, since the wife is the personal property of the husband" (Babylonian Talmud, sixth tradition).

Other sayings of the Ten Curses included:

- *"Her head is covered like a mourner; and it is not shaved except on account of immorality."*
- *"Her ear is pierced like [the ears of] perpetual slaves."*
- *"Like a hand-maid she waits on her husband."*
- *"She ceases to give birth while men never cease being able to beget children."*
- *"She stays in the home and does not show herself in public like a man (is confined to a prison)."*
- *"When she goes out into the marketplace her head has to be covered like a mourner saying: 'We have brought death upon all the inhabitants of the world.'"*

Part of a Jewish man's daily prayer (under Talmud training) also included this recitation, *"Blessed are You, Lord our God, King of the universe Who did not create me a woman"* (Tosefta Berakhot 6:18).[20] According to Rabbi Yehuda, "A man is required to say three blessings every day: *"Blessed [is God] who did not make me a gentile, **blessed [is God] who did not make me a woman**, blessed [is God] who did not make me an ignoramus ... [one must say]."* [21]

Earliest sources say that the intention of this "blessing" was rooted in the idea that, since women were busy taking care of the home (and thus unable to attend Mishnah learning), it was better to be a man who was free to study God's Word. I appreciate the fact that today, I as a woman, can take care of my home and study God's Word!

The Talmud continued to be compiled over the next four-hundred years between Israel's captivity to the time of Christ, which is an era called the "period of silence." It was so called because there was no recorded voice of the prophets. How easily even God's people are prone to mix truth with pagan ideas when not listening to God...and thus, brew for ourselves ideas and traditions based in falsehood that prevail in religious culture.

As God's Son was preparing for His coming to earth, two more world influencers rose to the top. The first was Greece. Ah yes, the philosophers and thinkers! Let's see what they thought about women.

EXPLOITING EVE

As ancient Greek culture was beginning to transition, the identity of *Eve* as a child-bearer went to a new level in Sparta. Women weren't relegated to the home, but were allowed to train and participate in competitive games. The idea was that strong women could produce strong babies. Spartan woman could bear one man's child and still remain married to another. They could even be married to two or more men at the same time.

This unusual custom of Spartan life was called "wife sharing." Three, four, sometimes more, brothers might share the same wife as a means of preventing the dividing of their inheritance into several, much smaller parts through children. They regarded any child produced by the relationship as belonging equally to all. And finally, an unmarried man, wanting a child but not wanting the responsibility of a wife and home outside of his [military] barracks, might ask to "borrow" a wife for the purpose of producing a child.[22]

Obviously women kept very busy there.

GREEK MINDSETS GO GLOBAL

As the Persian Empire faded, the new Classical Greece (500-300 BCE) rose to prominence. Athens shone as the first ever democracy with power being held by an assembly of all the male citizens. Athens became renowned as the world's greatest center of philosophers, thinkers, poets, and writers that have influenced the world, even to today. It was a grand hub of learning, with sophists and philosophers traveling across Greece teaching rhetoric, astronomy, cosmology, geometry, and the like. It was also a culture laced with philosophical misogyny.

Many philosophers today concede that Greek culture and philosophy has influenced much of Western thought since its inception, and, in fact, is "considered to be the seminal culture which provided the foundation of modern Western culture."[23]

The influence of Greek culture and philosophy flourished for two main reasons:

1. **Unification of language and culture**: During the Persian wars, Greece had come under Macedonian influence (though not control) through the League of Corinth formed by Philip, the father of Alexander the Great. It was Alexander's conquests, however, that permanently changed the Greek world as thousands of Greeks travelled with him, or after him, to settle in Greek cities newly founded through his advance. The most important of these was Alexandria in Egypt. Greek speaking kingdoms were established throughout Egypt, Syria, Iran and Bactria.[24]

2. **Methods were used that advanced ideas:** The Greeks effectively employed proven ways to advance ideas through writings, plays, poetry, education, and the arts. Through these methods, along with traveling teachers, Greek philosophy spread to Europe, Asia, and many parts of the Mediterranean region.

While this brought many benefits to the world in realms of education and government, it was also a means that continued to promote a low view of women.

REINVENTING A WOMAN'S IDENTITY

While other ancient cultures each had their own version of creation (often depicting the woman as merely an "afterthought" or as a "favor to man"), the Greek version viewed the woman as "being created as a form of punishment." In Greek mythology, it's said she was designed by the gods with "outward beauty to be irresistible to men," but with "inward characteristics that would deliberately bring sorrow, harm and trouble to man." [25]

Like all ancient cultures, Greeks also believed that childbearing was a woman's primary role. Otherwise, wives were ignored and confined to the back part of the house. Only slave-girls, harlots, concubines, and the very poor were free to wander about. Women were forbidden to own much property or to inherit it. Any business deal had to be with the approval of her guardian if the value was above a small sum. An heiress had no say in the selection of the husband who was going to manage her inheritance. Anything she inherited passed to her son as soon as he came of age.

Women were not allowed to vote or to participate in the assembly. Most women were considered to be the ward of the men in their lives and their status was deplorably low. They were not expected to read or write, and in fact it was considered "*a terrible thing to do!*"[26]

Athenians viewed women as "deceptive creatures capable of causing harm to themselves and others...they were viewed as weaker in mind and body than men." Many believed that young girls were somewhat wild and difficult to control and that virgins were subject to hallucinations that could encourage them to be self-destructive. The solution was an early marriage because only by having a baby could she be a "fully-operational female."[27]

I'm showing you these cultural views (I know, deplorable, sorry) to later show you that these were the cultural mindsets the Apostle Paul had to confront on his missionary journeys into these regions!

THE ART OF PHILOSOPHIZING

Greeks advanced the low view of a woman's state through what I call "gender philosophy." It was bad enough creating dark laws and codes about women, but esteemed philosophers now wove misogynistic views of women into their teaching disciplines. This validated such ideas as being authentic truths. Misogyny refers to the discrimination, denigration, violence against, or sexual objectification of women.

Yes, *Abbadon* was continuing his campaign of enmity.

I'd say the following views are so absurd that they are laughable, but the fact is, they were shared views by many! Here is an excerpt from a commentary with quotes from the infamous Hippocratic School of Medicine:[28]

"The Hippocratic School [of medicine] presented men and women as separate species...While men's bodies were hot, dry, and compact, women's bodies were cool, moist, and spongy...thus, women lacked the firm control of bodily boundaries that men had. Women changed shape during pregnancy, and they leaked: blood, tears, and emotion. 'Since woman does not bound herself, she must be bounded. This is achieved by organization of her space, prescription of her gestures, ordering of her rituals, imposition of headgear, attendants, and other trappings'.

'Women are pollutable, polluted, and polluting in several ways at once...' The Greeks thought that women were especially unable to control their sexuality and natural body processes and so affected the world around them, potentially 'polluting' it.

Female pollution was contained not so much in tangible products, 'but in the intangible, in...female speech and in feminine gaze...Much of what is contained in the area of the female head [was] seen as inherently polluting. The mouth, eyes, ears, and hair [were] seen as potentially disruptive and dangerous areas of female contamination.' (Llewellyn-Jones:262). This is because of the belief that women had hollow tubes (bodoi) that went through their bodies, one end at the mouth, and

103

one at the genitals...Therefore, the head and genitals were directly connected and both had to be controlled by veils and clothing.... Women's veils came in a variety of forms to conceal the head to varying degrees. One of the most common veils was the kredemnon (head-binder)...'which both safeguards women's chastity and protects men from the debilitating dangers and pollution of female sexuality....' Women's voices too were seen as an evil disposition. 'Thus, while women in public were ideally silent, women's voices played an important part in Greek ritual.' This pertained to her part during the ritual of animal sacrifice. As the priest cut the throat of the victim, women uttered the high, piercing cry known as the ololyge at the 'crucial moment of mediation between mortals and gods.'"

"Great Thinkers" on Women

Greek philosophers have influenced the world on many ideas. While Plato seemed to affirm women's potential as a valid contributor to the working society outside the home ("a reasoning that stood in contrast against the unreasonable treatment of women in his day"), yet he also advocated a system of "communal wives" (perhaps as Sparta had done).

Aristotle, however, was a true representative of Greek thought: "**keep the women secluded and uneducated.**" He contended that "women exist as natural deformities or imperfect males and are inherently inferior," and "the love between men and women are lesser and destined solely for the procreation of offspring."[29]

A few examples of what these esteemed masterminds penned include:[30]

Aristotle: "Man is by nature superior to the female and so the man should rule and the woman should be ruled."(Aristotle, *Politics*).

Demosthenes: "We keep hetaerae [harlots] for the sake of pleasure, female slaves for our daily care and wives to give us legitimate children and to be the guardians of our households" (Demosthenes, *Apollodorus Against Neaera*, III, 122). What is bizarre is that hetaerae (a prostitute with a courtly, wealthy, or upperclass clientele) were permitted free access to learning and almost all pursuits while the mothers of Athenian citizens were condemned to ignorance and anonymity.

Euripides: [described as the most intellectual poet of his time and a great Greek tragedian] is said to have a "certain hatred for women" and lived in a time when misogyny was a cultural norm in Classical Greece.[31] His works reflected how Athenian culture often thought of women by giving his characters such dialogue as: *"I am only a woman, a thing which the world hates,"* (Phaedra, speaking in Euripides' *Hippolytus*). *"No cure has been found for a woman's venom, worse than that of reptiles. We are a curse to man"* (Andromache, speaking in Euripides' *Andromache*). Euripides also wrote in his book, *Meda, "If women didn't exist, human life would be free of all its miseries."*

Hipponax (still quoted today): *"There are two days on which a woman is most pleasing – when someone marries her and when he carries out her dead body"* (Hipponax).

There is power in the written and spoken word, and Greek culture used it purposefully and creatively, and in so doing, empowered many societal ways of thinking, including views about the female gender. Why did this matter? **Because ideas create culture, and the ideas that carry the most influence do so because they are written, taught, and exemplified through the arts.**

In other words, the power of the arts, media and education heavily sway the mindsets that drive the culture of a nation and its people. These, and other "cultural mountains," must be reconciled to heaven's designs if a society is to prosper with life and health – spiritually, mentally, relationally and emotionally.

105

THE COMPLETE FORGETTING OF GOD

At the death of Alexander the Great, the Macedonian Empire was divided to four generals, and with this event, the classical era of Greece transitioned to the Hellenistic era (323 BCE). Hellenism was a fusion of the Ancient Greek world with that of the Near East, Middle East and Southwest Asia. It was a further departure from *barbarian* cultures, but with it came the rise of a new philosophy—*Humanism*.

Hellenistic civilization flourished from Central Asia to the western end of the Mediterranean Sea as a wave of Greek colonization established Greek cities in Asia and Africa. Greek culture and power was at its peak and continued to prosper throughout Europe and Asia, carrying its influence through the arts, exploration, literature, theatre, architecture, music, mathematics, philosophy, and science. The main cultural centers expanded from mainland Greece to Pergamum, Rhodes, and newly founded Greek colonies such as Seleucia, Antioch, and Alexandria.

The philosophy of Humanism spread as the crown of intellectual thought in which man defined himself as the center of all things. It touted that the power to think and reason gives man his worth and that there is no higher authority than reason. It promoted that "God" is an abstract idea and not a personal presence. It also taught education as being male-oriented, while girls were trained just for raising children.

Greeks were first to use abstract thought to explore life's big questions of: who am I? Where did I come from? What is right and wrong? What is the meaning of life? Sophistic teachers focused on rhetoric while rejecting the idea of single universal truth. They stressed civic duty and excellence in all things.[32]

This is the world into which Paul, just a few years down the line, took his missionary journeys. This is why knowing this regions background helps us understand some of Paul's dialogue with the newborn churches he established within Greek civilization. With what you have just read you can imagine the issues and questions that arose. We will look at these more, later. You will be happily surprised!

EMPIRES OF MEN

And finally, we can't close this chapter without mentioning the other world influencer, the most renowned culture on earth that ushered in the birth of Christ—Rome. Though Rome was influenced by Greek culture, it had its own longstanding influence on the development of language, religion, architecture, philosophy, law, and forms of government. Roman women had always experienced somewhat more freedom, voice, and personal development, and thus influence, than their Greek counterparts. Roman men placed a strong value on marriage, home, and the family and this made a difference on how women were treated, though women were still considered inferior and often sold and bought like merchandise, too.

At the beginning of the Empire, Emperor Augustus had tried to introduce a series of laws to promote more "traditional values" (female restrictions), but there was a tide of progress in motion for women's freedom that even he couldn't stop. The wind of heaven was beginning to blow and soon the great Liberator of men's souls would appear...the Last Adam.

CULTURAL VIEWS SHAPE PERSONAL VIEWS

The views we've read in this chapter have not been from one or two cultures, but a collective voice revealing a world current, including other places not mentioned. This powerful stream that impacted gender relationships reflected the serpent's enmity and exploitation of a fallen desire-rule paradigm. Eating from the tree of the knowledge of good and evil created a judgment culture and an abysmal disunity between men and women.

It was into this setting that the gospel of the Kingdom of heaven came.

Statistics show that women who live under oppression and abuse often believe it to be right...though it is not. Likewise, women held in religious bondage often believe it to be acceptable...but it is not. Cultural traditions, whether social, religious, or family, have a way of shaping our perspectives and views of life, including our personal identity. They shape how we see our worth, value, and purpose, and thus impact our choices...and even the development of our entire life.

God wasn't indifferent to the helper's plight. Rather, He was deeply moved at the darkness He witnessed tearing at the fabric of all mankind's soul. He longed for His sons and daughters, for the redemption of the *Yod* and the *Hey* whom He had created in His image. It was time to send the serpent-head Crusher.

- 6 -

REDEEMING EVE

*"There came a time when the risk to remain tight in the bud
was more painful than the risk it took to blossom."*

— *Anais Nin*

Onto the stage of a fallen world, Jesus entered — the
promised Seed, born of a virgin, just like the prophecies
foretold since the beginning. He would crush the
serpent's head. This triumphant One was born into a Jewish home
under Roman rule, surrounded by a Greek speaking culture. He
saw clearly mankind's bondage and depravity, including the
hostile journey of *Eve*. He came as the Great Apostle, the divine
Yod, to reclaim the earth with His Father's Kingdom. He would
restore the identity of men and women back to original design as
the fiery kings and priests over their appointed territories.

The serpent-head Crusher emerged to reunite the heart of
humanity with the heart of the Creator, *and* with good will toward
one another. And what's more, He would heal the breach between

the genders created at the Fall, and doing so, they would shine as the unified government of *Elohim's* image once again.

This Man of Holy Fire would destroy *Abbadon's* rule along with his chaos. As the *Prince of Peace*, He would bring rest to the earth.

I love how the Ruler of the Nations humbled Himself, to such degree, so as to make His first appearance in this world, of all places, in the womb of a woman—perhaps the most exploited environment created by the Fall. This realm of Eve's identity, broken and bruised in a judgment paradigm, was the first place His grace came to.

EVE MEETS THE LAST ADAM

The Last Adam came as a Father honoring, woman respecting, garden protecting, covenant carrying *Yod*. He came to do the Father's will and He wasn't passively standing around watching the devil manipulate someone and not doing anything about it, or worse, agreeing with it.

This Holy Spirit-filled Last Adam went from town to town setting people free from the devil's works and wiles. Chains of demonic oppression fell off those who encountered Him. He countered cultural thinking, family customs, political correctness and religious traditions. He exposed mindsets that denied love and shut out the Kingdom of Heaven.

Interestingly, the ones who opposed Him most were the Talmud-quoting, religious leaders…those steeped in religious tradition. Some of these traditions, as we saw in the last chapter, were stained with Babylonian and Greek cultural ways of thinking, especially regarding women.

But Jesus, the divine Teacher who taught with authority, was different in His views, including His perspective of the female gender. He thought what His Father thought about them. He didn't cast stones or cover women's heads with religious shame by His words. Nor did He relegate women to some back room with disdain. Instead, here are just a few ways that Jesus defied cultural norms of His day in affirming God's love for the daughters:

Jesus included women in His company: Though women normally stayed home and did domestic duties, Jesus allowed many women (some of them prominent) to travel with Him and His twelve disciples including: Mary Magdalene, Mary (mother of James and Joses), Salome, Joanna, and Susanna. Some were even at the crucifixion when most of the disciples had run away in fear (Matt. 27:55-56; Mark 15:40-41; Luke 8:1-3).

Jesus spoke with women: In John 4, we see Jesus speaking to a Samaritan woman at a well, asking her for some water. "Proper" Jews did not speak to women or Samaritans, and certainly not to a Samaritan woman. It was culturally unacceptable! But Jesus' conversation not only led to her conversion, but she became the first apostolic evangelist. History records her as St. Photini who brought many to Christ. Later, she travelled to Carthage because of the persecution against Christians but continued in ministry. There, under Nero's reign, she was martyred for the sake of the gospel.[1]

Jesus encouraged women to learn: Jewish women were generally not educated or allowed to even be so by this time in their culture—a tradition promoted by the Talmud. Nevertheless, Jesus encouraged Mary to learn from Him with the rest of the men instead of sending her off to the kitchen—the usual woman's place. Jesus also let Mary's sister, Martha, know that she had the freedom to do the same (Luke 10:39-42).

Jesus rescued women from social injustice: Some religious leaders wanted to stone a woman caught in adultery, yet her male companion was not brought to trial with her (John 8:2-11). Everyone knew that ancient law stated both guilty parties were to have been brought for sentencing (Lev. 20:10). Jesus, however, wrote something on the ground that caused them to drop the rocks they had ready to stone her. He set a standard of both justice and mercy. He extended to her forgiveness as well as a fatherly correction.

Jesus healed women who were social outcasts: Jesus didn't only heal leprous men who stood as social outcasts, but women too, including the woman with the issue of blood (which also made her a social outcast—Luke 8:43-48).

Jesus respected women's prophetic gifting: At the wedding in Cana, His mother saw in the Spirit that it was time for Jesus to walk in signs and miracles. At first, even He didn't think it was time, but realized she was correct in what she was seeing and turned the water into wine for the feast (John 2).

Jesus revealed Himself first to a woman after His resurrection: It wasn't to one of His disciples that He revealed Himself after He rose from the dead, but to a woman—Mary Magdalene (Mark 16:9).

Two of Jesus' three closest friends were women: Mary, Martha, and Lazarus. He honored all three as beloved friends.

And while Jesus' last words *before* His death were to His mother and disciple John, His first words *after* the resurrection were to a woman (John 19:26-27; Mark 16:9). The *Yod* was, again, setting a new precedent in restoring the value of the daughters. In other words, Jesus did NOT promote female suppression in a world of men. He demonstrated the worth of both male and female as God's image and delight. It was this identity He came to restore.

THE LAST ADAM RESTORES IDENTITY

Brokenness and sin had become mankind's identity. *Identity* means: the distinct characteristics of an individual by which they are known. *Sin* means: to err, to miss the mark as an arrow to the target. Humanity stood as a creation that had missed the mark of divine calling...but then came Jesus, the identity restorer. He would return the holy flame within mankind to once again be arrows in the Father's quiver for hitting the mark of divine purpose.

This holy *Yod* of manifest love walked in faithful obedience to God. He lived with holy backbone, drawing His strength from the deep well of His Father's love. He knew His identity—one that was not defined by man, but by Abba Father!

He stood among the crowds declaring, "I am the Way, the Truth, and the Life...I am the Bread of Heaven come down." He knew His Father, His mission, and His identity, and He walked in it...without fear. He never let go of it or exchanged it for another. The intimate understanding of His identity and personhood was anchored deep within Him—deep within His unity with Abba.

His declarations were not words springing from self-importance or arrogance, but were a verbal agreement with God's designs in Him, for Him, and through Him.

This serpent-head Crusher fulfilled prophetic promise by giving His life as a sacrificial Lamb to pay the penalty of our sin. He took our eternal death sentence upon Himself on the cross, taking every bit of our sin, shame, brokenness, and death. He took the curse and judgment that belonged to us, allowing God's wrath to fall on Himself for our sake.

In other words, **He ended the edict of our altered design incurred at the Fall**.

The Last Adam did what the first man failed to do—love God with all his heart, soul, mind, and strength, and minister reconciliation of the earth to Father's designs. He offered Himself as the *gateway* to our full restoration.

Jesus' humility lauded Him as the Head of a new host of humanity—the redeemed! The redeemed are whoever will accept a New Covenant with God in the Last Adam. These have a new identity with fully restored purpose. Being children of Light as the healed and restored ones is the identity by which we are to be known on earth, and before the heavens.

THE NEW CREATION

In Christ, we have an identity to walk in without fear and with holy backbone. It may be contrary to some of our cultural norms, family customs or political correctness, but as someone once said, "Just because something is, doesn't mean it should be so." The holy fire within Christ ignites us, as His Body, to live anchored and undaunted for our Father's Kingdom...even to the laying down of our lives.

Jesus fully dealt with the imprecation of our covenant breaking on the cross. And after three days in the underworld, setting captives free even there, the Father raised Jesus back to life by the Spirit of Holiness. In His hands were the keys of the Kingdom that had once belonged to mankind—His death had won them back. Now He offers them to us.

His resurrection stands today as a radical invitation to us to step out of a fallen nature with its judgment, and step into a New Covenant relationship with God as a new creation in Him, the Last Adam. **His life is our invitation to transformation**—one of being conformed to His same image as doorways to the supernatural supply of heaven for earth...with keys in our hands!

"Therefore if anyone is in Christ, he is a new creature; the old things passed away; behold, new things have come." (2 Corinthians 5:17)

This *new creation and doorway identity* redefines our entire life. We learn a completely new way of thinking as sons and daughters of God. We learn to shed barbaric customs as well as humanistic, Hellenistic, and Pharisaical mindsets. Under the mentoring of the Holy Spirit and through the revelation of God's Word, we gain a new mind...Christ's. As we experience intimacy with Him, we become a fiery, face-to-face, counterpart to the Last Adam.

We are no longer trapped in Abbadon's lair, nor in the strongholds of our own thinking. We can now shed Eve's rags as we redress in *Ishshah's* governmental robe!

Truth came to set us free and bring us back into the empowered design of *Elohim's* image. We are free from the yoke of another's opinion determining our worth. Men and women alike are called to remove the chains of an altered design and embrace one another in a restored paradigm of glory, and thus unity.

THE EMANCIPATION PROCLAMATION

The life and work of the Last Adam opened a whole new era of Kingdom empowerment. Yes, women too were included in the Holy Spirit's activity in the earth. Jesus said, "If the Son makes you free, you will be free indeed [indeed – in reality, as opposed to what is pretentious, fictitious, false, or hypothetical]" (John 8:36, clarification mine).

Jesus made the way for His Bride, a united body of men *and* women, to live as His counterpart in doing the works of the Father. He "went to sleep" for an empowered *helper* full of His same Spirit to come forth! And His Bride would not be a silent partner!

In the new day of redemption women were welcome in religious services. They were prophesying, learning, and ministering right along side the men. The cross and resurrection thundered the greatest emancipation proclamation ever, for all mankind. It was a new day on earth. The way was open to return to original design and authentic dominion.

Some say that Jesus seemed to favor men, after all, His chosen twelve were men, and it was to them that He said, "I appoint to you a kingdom, as my Father appointed to Me" (Luke 22:29). First of all, He did have women within the circle of disciples who were close to Him. However, He specifically chose twelve men to train

115

in a new Kingdom paradigm. Twelve is the number of government and He was establishing a new government on the earth. It was imperative that they "get it."

In searching for a clear answer to this question of why He only chose men, I've read anything from it being "culturally correct" (since they travelled over night, thus it was necessary to protect a woman's reputation who might otherwise have been involved in these journeys), to the fact that women were typically caring for family and would have been unavailable on the spot, etc. However, I believe the reason is simple.

God, from the beginning, established His paternal image as the "point man" and catalyst in divine purpose. Jesus, in regards to the earth and Church, is Father's "Point Man," and He chose twelve men to begin the work of re-establishing heaven's dominion on earth. But here it is: *God started with men, but it didn't stop with men!* Just like in the garden.

These twelve were learning, through an intense training from Jesus, a restored paradigm in the midst of a fallen world. And under His mentoring, they were learning to embrace women with His perspective of them as God's image, too. And when the Spirit came, women were included as fully empowered co-laborers. *Ishshah* was given her place to rise again and stand tall!

We call this respecting the sovereignty of God in "allowing" Him to do His work in His way! Jesus may have started with twelve men, but they became the catalyst of a whole family of apostles, prophets, pastors, teachers, and evangelists consisting of both men and women. Jesus trained twelve men to think in a completely different way than their Talmud upbringing in a Greco-Roman world. He trained them to be fathers who would release not just sons, but the mothers and daughters into fullness.

It's okay if He starts with a man, but we get included too! We aren't shut out. We need to let God do things the way He wants and not twist its meaning...not create an interpretation of being something He never intended.

116

For too long, some leaders have used "Jesus' Twelve" as a standard to hold women out of certain areas of ministry. While empowered godly women don't compete or vie for platforms, we do—like the daughter of Caleb in Judges 1—look to our Father and say, "Give me my blessing and inheritance!" As holy women, we want our promised jubilee.

WOMEN ENDUED WITH POWER

When the 120 waited in the Upper Room for the promised Holy Spirit, **both men and women were there, receiving the outpouring of the Holy Spirit and fire that marked the birth of the Church** (Acts 2:3-4). It wasn't just twelve men anymore. It was the return of divine fire to the spirit of the male and female rulers! The promise of the Father was for women too, just as it is today (Acts 1:8). And with the Spirit came gifts!

Women were also anointed to preach the gospel, heal the brokenhearted, proclaim liberty to captives, heal the blind, and free the oppressed (Luke 4:18). Just as God called the first male and female "Adam," so too, God sees us as one with Christ to co-labor with Him regardless of our gender.

In Mark 16:17-18, Jesus said, *"These signs will accompany those who have believed: in My name they will cast out demons, they will speak with new tongues; they will pick up serpents, and if they drink any deadly poison, it will not hurt them; they will lay hands on the sick, and they will recover."*

So, what part of "those who have believed" is gender restrictive?

None!

One of the most memorable moments in my life was when I was 11 years old. The year was 1969, and it was during the early stages of a fresh global outpouring of the Holy Spirit. One evening, my parents went with some friends to a home meeting. When they returned my mother's face was glowing. It's the only way I can describe it! I looked at her and said, "What happened to you? Whatever it is, I want it!" Over the next week we studied the scriptures and I learned about the person of the Godhead called Holy Spirit.

The following week I went and I also received this wonderful promise from the Father. It was a woman who led the meeting, and as she gently laid her hands on my shoulders she prayed, "Lord, fill this little lamb with Your Holy Spirit." I instantly felt as if I were sitting on the Heavenly Father's lap, embraced by His strong and loving arms. As I praised, I also received my prayer language.

That experience launched my life into a new realm of intimacy with God and deep hunger for His presence. It was the beginning of a new day, though not absent of warfare from the *whisperer* who wanted to stop my advancement in God.

The Holy Spirit does not limit Himself, His gifts, or His power to one gender. While we refer to Holy Spirit as "He," even the Hebrews understood that God is not male, but in Him are both the paternal and maternal qualities and attributes. In fact, the Hebrew word for *"Holy Spirit"* is *"Ruach Hachodesh"* and is a feminine noun.

What those believers on the day of Pentecost, 2,000 years ago, experienced in relationship with the Holy Spirit was just the beginning for the Body of Christ. Today, the Holy Spirit continues to move and empower Christ's Body with gifts and power, miracles, administration, healing, and teaching for the healing of the nations. Unfortunately, we've lost centuries of maturing in the things of God because of false doctrines that deny God's power for today and limit Christ's Body—limiting both men and women—in spiritual development.

Similar to the journey of women, Christ's own spiritual Bride has suffered silencing, subjugation and persecution at the hands of men...and not just by world systems, but by religious doctrines like Cessationism.

118

Shortly after my family received the baptism of the Spirit, our pastor began a six-week series denying the baptism of the Spirit for today. "What was experienced in Acts was for then, not now," he said. After this we were given the left foot of fellowship, but that was okay. My parents were on fire and began holding prayer and Bible studies weekly in our home that continued over the next few years. God's presence was tangible and many would experience healing, deliverance, and a new touch from God. Ministers from all over the nation came to teach in our gatherings. Friends and people from neighboring cities came hungry to know a deeper life in God through this wonderful person of the Godhead called Holy Spirit!

WOMEN AND SPIRITUAL GIFTS

While some argue that there were no women apostles or pastors in the New Testament, the truth is there were! There were not as many as men, because in general, women were busy raising families—nurturing sons and daughters and training them for the purpose of God in their life.

The early church followed Jesus' example in including women. Some of those named in the New Testament included Jesus' mother, Mary, as well as Dorcas, Julia, Lydia, Persis, Tryphena and Tryphosa. Paul gratefully acknowledged women who served *with* him as co-laborers in ministry and leadership— women such as Phoebe, Junia and Priscilla who helped lay foundations in the early church.

Paul expressed his solidarity with women leaders such as Euodia and Syntyche, and in his letters he referred to other women who led churches, such as Chloe and Nympha.[2]

Sometimes we have been more concerned about the *gender* of someone God is using in ministry than the fact that it is *GOD* who is using the vessel! We often qualify or disqualify people on the basis of gender, age, or race, rather than receiving the gift of God's presence and anointing in their life. We perceive them by the flesh rather than knowing them by the Spirit.

Spiritual gifts and offices are determined and given by God, not people: *"And **God** has appointed in the church, first apostles, second prophets, third teachers, then miracles, then gifts of healings, helps, administrations, various kinds of tongues"* (1 Cor. 12:28). God is the distributer of His gifts. And since there is "neither male nor female" in Him, gender doesn't determine what gift He gives you (Gal. 3:28).

In Ephesians 4:8-12, we are told that Jesus gave gifts to *"men"* (Grk. *"anthropos"*). This word means: male *or* female mankind. And this scripture is specifically talking about apostles, prophets, pastors, teachers, and evangelists!

In 1 Peter 4:10-11, the apostle Peter taught that *all* believers are to serve others with whatever gift God has given them. If God gave a woman the gift of being a pastor or teacher, then she is expected by God to exercise that gift!

Some of the other spiritual gifts listed in scripture are: prophecy, service, teaching, counseling, generosity, leadership, mercy, word of wisdom, word of knowledge, gift of faith, gift of healing, working of miracles, discernment of spirits, tongues, and interpretation of tongues (Rom. 12; 1 Cor. 12). And in the age of the Holy Spirit, both the sons and the daughters are given gifts and all are empowered to "prophesy" (Acts 2:17).

While gifts are not the source of our identity, they play a critical role in walking out our identity in Christ.

DISMANTLING RELIGIOUS MINDSETS

One time, a dear friend of mine shared with me her own journey of discovering God's truth for her as a woman. She said for years she walked in a dominant place in her marriage while her husband had a more passive role. She sensed that wasn't God's order for their home, so she took the opposite stance and pushed him to the front as "the leader" while assuming a passive place under his ruling.

She stopped using her gifts and assumed a demure position, feeling that was the "proper" way a Christian marriage should operate. But after a few years, she realized that wasn't working either! Squelching one's gifts in order to fit a *traditional* role doesn't work, nor is it what our Father desires.

It wasn't until they both realized that they were to lead together in unity, that the marriage began to function the way God intended—both flourishing in their gifts with unified vision for their home, work, and ministry. They realized that living by the fallen design of a *desire-rule* paradigm was embracing a judgment pattern, which it was NOT God's plan for a redeemed couple! Original design that's restored in Christ is what God desires.

As I said earlier, because of the false teaching my family received when I was young, I saw my mother do the same thing. She was a feisty go-getter, but squelched some of her gifts while trying to make my dad the sole leader and priest—*you* make the decisions...be the spiritual boss...*you* be the voice. But stifling her life and pushing my father to step up to the plate of a pre-redemption desire-rule model was a brew for false control and frustration...on both sides.

Even the apostles themselves had to shed cultural ideologies regarding women as they learned to release them into their full calling in Christ. Peter taught men to *honor* their wife as a fellow *heir of grace* (1 Peter 3:7). And this wasn't merely about honoring their salvation experience, but the gifts they received from God "according to the grace given them."

The apostles learned from the Master that women too were joint heirs with men...in marriage and outside of marriage.

Divine instruction taught that marriage was not to squelch a woman's gifts and call of God.

121

I know women today who have to ask a husband's permission for everything they do, because they feel it is what the Bible teaches. I read an article recently arguing about whether a woman even has the right to go to the bathroom without asking her husband. We may think this is absurd (and it is!), but it's obviously a sad reality for some. When a woman engages a false kind of submission to a man, even giving him priority above her submission to God, she makes him her idol. And when a man establishes his control as a priority over a woman's freedom in Christ, he makes himself an oppressor. In a redeemed marriage, there is no control. There is only love and honor.

Control and false submission negate healthy communication and needed discussion. I talk to my husband about everything because we are one! I never feel controlled by him...only loved.

PARADIGM OF EMPOWERMENT

Jesus established a paradigm of empowerment. He confronted the Talmud-quoting religious leaders of His day, condemning the way many of them suppressed people while taking seats of honor for themselves.

He said, *"They tie up heavy burdens and lay them on men's shoulders...they do all their works to be seen of men...woe to you, scribes and Pharisees, hypocrites, because you shut off the kingdom of heaven from people; for you do not enter in yourselves, nor do you allow those who are entering to go in"* (Matt. 23:4-13).

What's more, Jesus didn't say this behind closed doors to a few close disciples, but to the multitudes where every one could hear! He wanted them to know—*religious bondage is not the Father's will!*

While Jesus' disciples wrangled about superiority and chief places, He rebuked their line of thinking saying, "You know that the rulers in this world lord it over their people, and officials flaunt their authority over those under them. *But it shall not be so*

122

among you: but whosoever will be great among you, let him be your minister [servant]" (Matt. 20:25-26, NLT, emphasis and clarification mine). And Jesus meant this for every area of leadership—in society, in the fellowship of believers, and in the home.

Leaders are to empower others through serving them, enabling and helping them to prosper, and lifting them into divine destiny. Leadership and headship are designed to be a catalyst for creative flourishing, not a catacomb of control.

Even when Jesus rebuked devils and cast out demons, His treatment of people was one of love. Harsh words were never directed toward women or the common person, even when correcting them. However, severe words were used in addressing religious spirits!

Everything in our Father's Kingdom serves to empower another for fruitfulness that glorifies God.

LIVING AS MRS. LAST ADAM

Every day we are impacted by numerous ideologies and philosophies that push and pull us from all sides, each one vying for a seat of honor in our belief structure. Media, peers, television, fashion, culture and religious models (to name just a few) all carry their own message to influence how we should live and define our existence.

The messages we receive today are at an all time high, motivating how we eat, the choices we make, and how we interact with others. And unless we are rooted in God's love *and* truth, we will listen and believe what they say is true.

As women, we often seek affirmation through what we do, how we look, what others say about us, what culture tells us, and how we are treated by others. We battle the murk of self-talk, negative experiences, and difficult situations, trying to find a better us, an acceptable us...a loved and valued us.

123

But there is only one who can define us, and He created us to be a house of life as His *Ishshah*. He wants a Bride who dances with the sword of truth in intimacy with Him in authentic identity. The Last Adam emerged as the Mediator of a new, eternal, covenant with God. As such, we are restored to original design and calling...and more!

In Christ, we, as believers, are spiritual sons to Abba Father because the *Spirit of the Son* dwells in us. We are also Jesus' body (His Bride) who co-labors with Him for Father's purposes on earth. **Father sees us in the Son as one with Him** — not as being separate from Him, but having His same nature and spiritual DNA...just like He saw the original male and female together as Adam.

This realm of Sonship and Brideship is a deep mystery that isn't about physical body parts, but about the way we relate to God and the way He relates to us. As sons we experience Abba's love, parenting, and counsel for life and the work He gives us. We learn to live for our Dad (Abba), rather than for ourselves. As Christ's Bride, we experience union with Him as His suitable helper over territories, esteeming Him as preeminent, and bearing fruit that glorifies Father.

Do you see how critically important it is that we understand the original design of male and female that parallels our identity in Christ? Being fashioned "second" doesn't make us a lower being, rather, we are an affirmed Bride blessed and empowered for good works!

God designed men as powerful catalysts for His work on earth. The very order of creation gave a husband a divine responsibility to care for his body, his bone of his bone, and to prosper a bride. This isn't only regarding children, but with increase in every way for flourishing in all of her gifts!

How grateful I am for God's love to have sent the Son to redeem us out of a death paradigm and bring us into a grace paradigm of full living. He didn't extend such grace to Lucifer and the angels that fell with him, but He did it for us! God gave mankind the gift of redemption.

It's time to fully embrace the identity offered to us in Him, to see each other through His eyes as men and women of dignity, leadership, and a divine purpose.

- 7 -

CLARIFICATION, PLEASE!

*"For every complex problem there is an answer that is
clear, simple, and wrong."*

— H. L. Mencken

Every one of us has questions, and when searching for an answer, we will most often find one. But the key is in finding the *right* answer!

During the years of the early Church, letters written by the apostles circulated as needed counsel regarding the life of the new believer. Over the centuries, some began taking a few comments by Paul out of context, using them as a scriptural basis to repress a woman's value and place, especially in ministry—a dynamic not present in the early Church.

Paul's words were addressing specific issues present with new believers in a Greco-Roman culture. It has been misinterpretations of his words, even by honored theologians, that have led many in Christendom to place a false yoke on women.

Four verses alone have stood as the bar of prohibition against women from stepping into their full calling in God. These scriptures cover five critical topics: headship, submission, covering, silencing, and teaching (Eph. 5:22-23; 1 Cor. 11:2-16; 14:34-35; 1 Tim. 2:12).

Misinterpretations of these passages have kept many women from rising out of a fallen paradigm, both in the home and in the Church. And yet, there are *many* more verses that validate women as restored daughters of God...praying, speaking, teaching, and leading in a fully redeemed design. Genesis 3:16 (the judgment paradigm), has continued to be the model touted as "a woman's place" in many Christian teachings, rather than redemption and restoration to authentic design.

In this chapter, I want to clarify four of these areas, plus a few others. Headship will be covered more in-depth in a later chapter.

Every true teacher of the Word knows that to rest a doctrine on one verse alone becomes suspect, especially when the interpretation violates scripture as a whole. Paul's words were mostly written to new churches established in pagan cultures such as Corinth, Ephesus, Smyrna and Colosse. Remember, he was the apostle to the Gentiles—people who knew nothing of God and His ways. New converts were shedding cultural mindsets as they learned a NEW way of living as the Body of Christ.

As Paul took the light of the gospel to dark regions, he also brought correction to situations in the newly planted congregations. These corrections were based on specific incidents regarding both men and women. Though some of Paul's words make us think he was certainly "putting women in their place," his admonitions were NOT gender suppression! Rather, he was addressing wrong beliefs and behaviors hanging on from old lifestyles. I think we can all identify with that!

Remember, Greek philosophy, Humanism, Hellenism, myths, and idol worship dominated the Greco-Roman cultures that he visited, as we have already seen.

128

Paul taught the pure gospel that reconciles us to God and restores us to His image in Christ. Paul did NOT promote a gospel of condemnation in a continued fallen paradigm! Freedom from sin and empowerment of the Spirit for men and women were Paul's resounding themes as he preached the great news: *"You are all sons of God through faith in Christ Jesus... There is neither Jew nor Greek, slave nor free, male nor female, for you are all one in Christ Jesus"* (Gal. 3:26-28).

This anointed apostle spoke by the Holy Spirit as he trained up God's family in the earth. Each member, male and female, had gifts for ministry and service that were given (by God) and not based on gender, race or social status.

In recent years, some leaders have begun to address these important issues in scripture through the lens of Paul's true intent, as I will also do now. The Church must know the truth if we are to run, unhindered, in the course that God has for us—individually and together.

Let's look now at Paul's words to women and what they meant in Paul's mind and time. It's time to get some clarification!

LET WOMEN LEARN!

*"Let the woman learn in **silence** with all subjection. But I suffer
not a woman to teach, nor to usurp authority over the man,
but to **be in silence**."*
(1 Tim. 2:11-12, KJV, emphasis mine)

There are three important aspects to this verse. The first one is that Paul, in writing a letter to Timothy (pastor at Ephesus) said: **"Let the woman learn..."** Women were included in the learning environment of discipleship. This was completely contrary to most traditional settings where neither Jews nor Greeks found any value in educating women, and who even viewed it as a disgrace. Such prejudices had kept women in the dark, but Jesus changed that and Paul was following suit. However, there was obviously

an issue with some whose behavior was disruptive. This leads us
to the next point as it deals with cultural dynamics.

CUT THE DRAMA, GIRLS!

The second point to clarify is the next part of Paul's statement: *"in
silence."* In the original text, Paul did NOT imply that women were
to "be silenced," but to receive instruction *"quietly"* (Grk.
"hesychia"), **as opposed to being loud and disruptive.** I know it's
hard to believe that women could be loud, opinionated, and
disruptive, but apparently some women in Ephesus were very
much so!

Some historical records indicate that an ancient tribe of
"warlike" women from Asia helped to establish the beginnings of
Ephesus. These women were warriors, rulers, and priestesses, as
well as domestics, alongside the men of their tribe. Myths,
however, portrayed them as an all female society that held women
to be *far superior* to males, who made slaves of men, using them
only for their own proliferation (keeping only female offspring).
These women were said to be so fierce that they cut off one breast
in order to shoot more quickly with their bow. Some studies,
however, show such myths to be more notion than reality.[1]
Nevertheless, whether truth or myth, the idea of female
superiority prevailed in Ephesus.

Now, put Paul's correction as a spiritual father into context of
what I just showed you about the domineering female mindset in
their culture. The term *"with all subjection"* referred to a person's
own use of *self-control*. The *woman* was to refrain herself from
disruptive outbursts. In other words, come and learn, but not like
an Amazon woman...which is what some seemed to be doing!

Devotion to these myths had inspired the practice of
genealogies that linked them to their domineering ancestors.
That's why Paul also corrected them saying, *"Have nothing to do
with irreverent, silly myths. Rather train yourself for godliness"* (1 Tim.

4:7, ESV). This belief of female-superiority was causing contention in the home and in gatherings. Paul had to correct their wayward devotion and instruct them to give attention to godly edification in faith.

In Ephesians 5, Paul writes another word of admonition to these superior-minded, warrior women to cooperate with their husbands, to "submit" themselves in loving cooperation. He wasn't advocating, however, that they should be walked over.

It is amazing how misconstrued some of Paul's words have been. Talk about making a mountain out of a molehill. Nevertheless, our warfare is not with flesh and blood, but with spiritual darkness. *Abbadon's* rule may be overturned, but he is still present and working where he is allowed. Unrighteous subjection of the female gender is one of his works to shut out the kingdom of God.

NO MORE DEVOURING!

Third, Paul corrected the cultural female-superiority of *"usurping authority over a man."* The word *"authority"* here (Grk. *"authenteo"*) **had nothing to do with godly teaching or giving righteous instruction**. This word means: *one who acts as an absolute master and exercises dominion on their own authority*. This verse is the only place in scripture to use this word *"authenteo"* — a word confirmed in Greek literature 67% of the time to carry a dark meaning as in "instigating or perpetuating a crime." Paul was referring to some women who were trying to instigate domination by wielding a "personal authority" over men in the gathering. This is a little different than a woman who is teaching the Word honorably under the anointing of the Holy Spirit, wouldn't you say?

Ephesus not only had a history of "Amazon women," but it was the worship center of the goddess Artemis. This cult fanned the flame of women superiority since Artemis was seen as "the mother-goddess from whom all life issued." Her worshippers claimed that woman (Eve) preceded man (Adam), and therefore, it was the man who had been deceived by the serpent, not the female. Paul then retells the events of creation to reveal *what really happened*, so that believers would know the truth and recognize these false teachings about the creation account.

"For Adam was first formed, then Eve. And Adam was not deceived, but the woman being deceived was in the transgression" (1 Tim. 2:13-14).

These verses do not mean that all women are prohibited from teaching because Eve was created second, or because she was misled. It was simply: "Let's put the account straight, people!" We must see what a perversion some have made Paul's words to mean. Such twisting has lasted through many centuries of Church culture.

I don't doubt that some, even now reading my words, will be unable to embrace the full truth of a woman's place in ministry. It may still feel "unbiblical" if your training has told you otherwise. However, I pray for the eyes of your understanding to be open to what God means in His Word. We have a work to do and Father needs His daughters in full position, and fully empowered, for the work He's called us to do.

The Church needs the bold voice of spiritual fathers *and* mothers to train the sons and daughters with wisdom for their divine purpose during their time on earth.

Since we have been discussing silencing, let's take a look at another letter Paul wrote to the Ekklesia (Church) in Corinth.

COUNTERING CULTURE

*"Let the **women remain silent**, they are not permitted to speak, rather let them be submissive as also the **LAW** says; and if there is something they want to know, let them ask their own husbands at home; for it is **shameful** for a woman to speak out in a congregational meeting." (1 Cor. 14:34-35, NKJV, emphasis mine)*

Okay, let's calm our blood pressure as we look at what he was talking about. Two key words are clear evidence that Paul was NOT preaching a divine command or advocating that women be silenced. Those two words are: *Law* and *shameful*. Paul was a preacher of the gospel; LAW and shame are not part of the gospel of Christ's Kingdom!

First, the word **"LAW"** here is the Greek word "Nomos" and means: *anything received by usage, custom, a law, or a command, a rule producing a state approved of God.* Paul was not referring to the Torah (the word of God given to Moses), but the *Talmud.* Here we are again...interpretations and traditions of men that do not necessarily carry the heart and mind of God.

Paul's words were a response to a letter sent from the Corinthian church, a congregation that was planted in the heart of a Hellenistic society. Paul was quoting a part of that letter that dealt with the silencing of women. Now remember, Paul had just instructed in chapter 11 that *all* believers (men and women) were to prophesy! It's really hard to prophesy in silence.

Paul's response to the idea of silencing women was an emphatic, *"What! Do you think God's word originated with you? Are you the only ones to whom it was given? If you claim to be a prophet or think you are spiritual, you should recognize that what I am saying is a command from the Lord himself"* (1 Cor. 14:35-36, NLT).

And what command from the Lord was that? That **ALL** should prophesy, both men and women...just let it be done in order, honoring and preferring one another. Those who have ever been in an open-mic gathering know that some form of order is needed.

Second, the word **"shameful"** is another clue that Paul was not quoting God's Word as a command to women, but was quoting someone else. There is NOWHERE in the entire Old Testament where God says it's shameful for women to speak. This word *"shame"* (Grk. *"aiskron"*) actually means: *"lewd, vile, filthy, indecent, foul, dirty and morally degraded."* Sound familiar?

133

This was Greek philosophy and Talmud talk...and Paul was confronting it, not endorsing it!

PERMISSION GRANTED

A friend once told me that growing up in a non-believing home, her lifestyle was radically changed when she came to Christ. However, she shared with me that as a non-Christian, she had never experienced gender limitations until she came into the Church!

God has gifted women in many areas, especially in the areas of communication and teaching. To repress her gifts has been part of Satan's manifest enmity against her. You could imagine the joy that women in the early church were experiencing as the Holy Spirit, and Spirit-filled brothers, were lifting women, wives, sisters, and daughters into destiny, encouraging their gifts to come alive. Spiritual fathers gave them permission to flourish in their identity in Christ.

This was new freedom for both men and women. And Paul didn't just correct women, he also confronted men regarding heresies and false teachings that some were bringing in. Both had to learn truth before teaching others, rather than spouting philosophies and self-confident assertions that had no basis, or were mixed with cultic ideologies (1 Tim. 1:6-7).

Paul never intended for his words to be a blanket prohibition against women everywhere and always. He was simply bringing fatherly correction to the maturing sons and daughters of God.

MODESTY GIRLS, PLEASE!

"In like manner also, that the women adorn themselves in modest apparel, with propriety and moderation, not with braided hair or gold or pearls or costly clothing, but which is proper for women professing godliness, with good works." (1 Tim. 2:9-10, NKJV)

134

Since some take these words to legalistic extreme, I want to comment on this verse as well, and also clarify the importance of Paul's words. Like a good spiritual father, Paul had to get practical with God's daughters, even about modesty. As a man, Paul knew that immodest attire doesn't simply draw a man's attention, but causes him to lust in his mind. It leads him down a path where a godly woman has no right to lead him.

Women have used clothing since time began to draw the attention of men. Paul was teaching them to find their affirmation in God's love, and let His indwelling glory be the source of their radiant beauty. All of Paul's teachings were faithful instruction to women converts who had never been schooled in God's ways, nor how to live as Abba's daughters.

Remember, women lead by influence and not just with words, but by our appearance and behavior, too. Paul was not squelching wholesome creative expression. Rather, he was exposing any link to idol-worship in their fashion, while calling out their true identity as royal daughters of God. And they needed to dress like it! Yes, fashion can be an idol and part of idol-worship.

These women were the beginning of a new generation of empowered women in Christ. Their full development as spiritual women was key to helping raise the Body of Christ to full maturity. They were women of dignity who were to dress with dignity. They had to leave the old behind. They had good works to do and they couldn't be causing men to stumble at the same time. Remember, women had been shut out from learning. Now they were invited to join the men and learn...just don't seduce them while you're sitting across from them! Pretty practical if you ask me.

It is the same today. Short skirts and low cut blouses may seem fashionable, but if the attire is leading men's minds to lust after us, we better go home and change clothes. There are a lot of things we can wear that are stylish, yet honors our Father and our identity as His royal daughters...as well as honoring our heavenly husband, Jesus. Like the women of Paul's day, we must understand our role as spiritual leaders in culture, and not let culture lead us.

HAVING BABIES IS NOT A SALVATION REQUIREMENT!

"Notwithstanding she shall be saved in childbearing, if they continue in faith and charity and holiness with sobriety."
(1 Tim. 2:15, KJV)

The last point I want to illuminate in Paul's letter to Timothy was what he meant regarding salvation and childbirth. Clearly, "saved in childbirth" does not mean having babies is a pre-requisite of entrance to the celestial realm! And every woman said, "Amen!" Remember that the worship of Artemis was prominent in Ephesus. Women esteemed Artemis as their *protector in childbirth*. She was their place of safety when so many things could go wrong in labor and birth. The word "*saved*" literally referred to their being *kept safe* in childbirth.

You can imagine how important Paul's admonition was for these women to put their trust in God in *every* area of their life, instead of in the empty arms of Artemis. Again, these people were learning a new way of living as believers. Paul was fathering their faith to trust God rather than idols.

It is amazing what I have read in Christendom on this topic, some believing that "only here in childbearing are women released from the stigma of sin...from being second-class citizens...and from the stigma of having caused the Fall."[2] And here I thought it was Jesus' blood that washes away *all* stain of sin.

VEILING—WE HAVE NO SUCH CUSTOM!

"But I want you to understand that Christ is the head of every man, and the man is the head of a woman, and

136

God is the head of Christ...But every woman who has her head uncovered while praying or prophesying disgraces her head, for she is one and the same as the woman whose head is shaved. For if a woman does not cover her head, let her also have her hair cut off; but if it is disgraceful for a woman to have her hair cut off or her head shaved, let her cover her head.... Judge for yourselves: is it proper for a woman to pray to God with her head uncovered? Does not even nature itself teach you that if a man has long hair, it is a dishonor to him, but if a woman has long hair, it is a glory to her? For her hair is given to her for a covering. But if one is inclined to be contentious, we have no such practice [custom], nor have the churches of God" (1 Corinthians 11:3-16).

Veiling is not a divine ordinance, yet some have used this scripture as a "divine order" for women. Some, even in other faiths, use this in saying that Christian women who do not veil are out of order. However, Paul was not at all advocating the use of veils. Again, we know that Paul's letter was a response to a letter sent to him about issues in the assembly there in Corinth.

First, Paul begins speaking about a cycle of headship: Christ to a man, man to a wife (NOT man to every women, as some men claim), and God to Christ. *It is a circle of empowerment.* Did you ever see Father control Jesus? Or Jesus control a man? But somehow when it comes to the woman we interpret it as "authoritative control" or "boss." Wrong!

Paul clearly unfolded a beautiful picture of how Christ, who is empowered by the Father (because that is what a head does), in turn empowers a man for his role as a husband, who in turn empowers his wife for the life she is meant to live in union with him as blessed, fruitful, and thriving. We will explore more on this in the pages ahead.

Second, the verses which follow this foundation of empowerment are, apparently, an excerpt from a letter that is contending for the use of veiling. Again, veiling was a common *cultural* practice that was never instituted by God. Paul's final response was: *A woman's hair is her covering, but if you want to argue about it, we have no such practice [custom], nor do the churches of God!* Paul was careful not to advocate man-made customs as divine ordinances.

The truth is, when a veil is mandated, it is not only a suppression of a woman to deny her face, but some of the ideology in this is to keep a man from lusting by hiding her face. We've already addressed modesty issues, but this is different. It negates the man's own responsibility to yield his mind to God regarding his thoughts. Mostly, however, this argument was rooted in the Greek philosophy that a woman's face and voice were "polluting." If a woman wants to use a veil in her faith, that is her own right. Nevertheless, a veil on a head does not constitute a pure heart, nor does God command women to veil.

THE TRUTH ABOUT SUBMISSION

And now for the word that married women often hear stressed in Christian culture, the word *submit*—you know, our "dutiful and docile place as women."

A few years ago, I was asked to teach on authority and submission in my local church. It was a Wednesday evening and the minute I announced my topic a woman immediately started to bolt for the door (as she later put it). The Holy Spirit told her to sit down and listen to what I had to say. She obeyed, though rather reluctantly. After the message she came up, grabbed my hand, shook it heartily, and with all smiles recounted how my words had set her free from a very dark prison of *false submission.*

"Wives, submit to your own husbands, as is fitting in the Lord"
(Colossians 3:18).

So what is the truth about this oft' abused word regarding submission? Let's see.

First, Paul wrote these words to two specific congregations, the one at Ephesus and the one at Colosse. We've already seen why he would say this in his letter to the Ephesians because of the "Amazon women" culture there. However, Colosse also had similar idol worship.

The city of Colosse was the cultic center of the goddess Cybele, another pagan deity of fertility similar to Artemis. She was "depicted as an exotic mystery-goddess in a lion-drawn chariot and accompanied with wild music, wine, and a disorderly ecstatic following." Wahoo! Can't you just imagine what kind of wild time the Colossian women had learning that religion? These were not demure pious women raised on the front pew and singing in the choir...they were party women just having come to Jesus! Practical discipleship says, "Honey, get down from the barstool and go home. Take care of the kids and your husband...and don't abuse him with your words."

Again, these were new converts in pagan cultures. That's right, no Bible in every hotel drawer, no church on every corner, no Christian conference filling the downtown stadium with well-known Christian speakers from around the world...just Paul, Timothy, and a few others pioneering a revolution with the Holy Spirit, laboring to bring cultures out of darkness and into the light of God's love.

Paul's emphasis, "...to your own husbands," was a father's heart for them to leave independent carousing and be unified with their spouse for the purpose of God for them and their marriage. Paul's words were certainly not confined to just Ephesus and Colosse, but are for all of us today!

Second, let's look at the meaning of the word "submit." Submit (Grk. "hypotasso") was a military term that meant: to arrange under as a troop; to station one's self under another, to appoint on one's own responsibility or authority, to assign a place, ordain. However, in a non-military use, it was a "voluntary attitude of cooperating, assuming responsibility, and carrying a burden." In other words, there is a *divine assignment* for a wife—a mission under the care, protection, provision and empowering love of a husband. Wives have a *sub*-mission in which we station ourselves, fully empowered with authority and supply to accomplish it. Even God called His bride, Israel, a "daughter of troops!" (Micah 5:1)

The picture of the woman's cooperation is a *freewill* act on her own part, not his subjugating her by force (i.e. "You *have* to obey me! I'm your boss!") It is a voluntary attitude of yielding to a husband's advice as opposed to self-will independence ("I'll do it MY way!"). This is done on the basis of a woman's own personal responsibility and authority. Her voluntary act of cooperation is NOT from a demand or an obligation, but is a willing act of honoring...the opposite of devouring and manipulating until his automatic response becomes the conflict-free resolve of, "Yes, dear."

A woman's work regarding family is important. She is to be empowered for her work in the home, but not restricted to the home. An empowered woman on a mission is a completely different paradigm than subjugation in a desire-rule model.

Can you see why Paul needed to instruct these women about cooperating with their husband about the home, and not dominating or undermining a husband's importance? A culture of love and respect is to work both ways. I hope you are seeing the need for these words without changing Paul's intentions. No one likes oppression, domination, or being undermined—not men or women.

Third, this freewill cooperation with a husband is "as is fitting in the Lord." Again, it's not complicated. In Paul's letter to the Ephesians, he deepens the beauty of a husband-wife relationship through the model of Christ and His Bride. Wholesome cooperation is always fitting; being a "doormat" is not. Abuse is not. Christ does not abuse His Bride, and neither does He ask a woman to submit herself to the abuse of a husband.

That would be NOT FITTING! The biblical pattern of marriage is love and honor.

There is NO foundation in scripture for women to engage a sense of "Christian obligation" or duty to stay in an abusive relationship.

If this is your situation, please get right counsel. And I will say, not every Christian leader will give you right counsel. Some pastors still operate under the curse paradigm regarding marriage and support a man's rule over a woman, even if it is abusive. This is not Father's way or heart regarding you. It is NOT a paradigm of redemption. A good Christian counselor will help you find the direction you need, and so will law enforcement agencies.

CALLING A HUSBAND "LORD"

1 Peter 3:6 is another scripture that sometimes gets misconstrued:

"Sarah obeyed [listened with action] Abraham, calling him lord."

First, as we saw in an earlier chapter, Sarah's words were a Hebrew term esteeming one who protected, provided for, and presided as master over the wellbeing of a household or estate. It was the same word God's people used in referring to Him for His bountiful care and intimate oversight! Again, it was a term of loving respect and honoring a husband for all the good he does, not about control and subjection as being "lorded" over.

It is the later translations (rather than original, classical meaning) of the Greek word here for "lord" (kyrios) that have created misinterpretations of this scripture through Hellenistic influences. Remember, Sarah spoke Hebrew, not Greek. Peter used a word that was, at the time, the closest to the Hebrew understanding for lord.

Second, Sarah spoke on her own accord. She wasn't mandated to call Abraham *lord*...as some teach! As we remember, God also told Abraham, "...whatever Sarah tells you, listen to

141

her." The word listen (Heb. *shama*) means obey! But this didn't mean for him to obey her every whim either!

We can get things so out of context and twisted in our thinking. Some have taken this literally and taught that wives should mindlessly obey their husband's demands, and even call him "lord." Again, Peter was instructing new believers about respect in marriage. Christians were in a time of persecution and it was important to be aware of doing what was right, and not behaving in such a way that might also bring negative attention — such that might lead to terrible consequences, or even loss of life.

For this reason Peter also said to not fear. Peter was not promoting doormat-obedience. Rather, he was promoting righteous behavior and safety.

Let me say here, there is greatness in both a man and a woman, and all greatness demands humility. Proverbs 15:33 teaches us that *"before honor, comes humility."* Just as we saw in the beginning, the *Yod* of power (man) was to lead as God's image through humility; likewise, the *Hey* of revelatory breath (woman) was to join in leading through humility.

Being redeemed isn't instant perfection. As we forsake fallen mindsets one of the greatest attributes of God's likeness we must learn to cultivate is humility and love toward one another. True greatness finds wings in selflessness; true leadership moves with divine strength when void of ego.

TRUE SUBMISSION IS FREEWILL

The true concept of submission is critical for us to understand if we are to prosper with authority in our divine calling. All true authority begins with true submission to God, listening to Him and moving with His Spirit — and this applies to both genders. Growing up, I sometimes saw movies and television programs that showed a husband spanking his wife, and was portrayed as an "appropriate" way of disciplining her. But a man hitting a woman is NEVER appropriate. That was not true or right submission.

Some have translated submission as "unconditional obedience," but not only is that incorrect, obedience is what children are to give parents. Fathers are to bring children into subjection, not a wife. Even when Paul said that men are to *rule* (Grk. "*proistemi*") their home, he didn't mean they were to walk around with a big stick and bark out orders for everyone to follow. "*Proistemi*" means to preside over as a protector or guardian, to give aid, care and attention for the wellbeing and prosperity of a place (1 Tim. 3:5). It was the same care that an overseer was to provide for the prospering of God people.

Did you know there is actually no place in the Old Testament where God specifically commands wives to submit to the husband? Gasp and faint. Really. Before the Fall, the only command given was: be fruitful, multiply, and have dominion...and don't eat from the tree of the knowledge of good and evil. There was no sinful nature so love and honor were a natural dynamic between the couple.

It was in the new day of return to God that redeemed mankind had to relearn God's ways. A wife's submission meant honoring a husband, just as a man was to love his wife.

My heart has been to bring revelation and clarification to these critical matters that govern in Christendom...to get to the right answer! Right answers are truthful answers that empower right action. Right answers nurture our full development as God's image on earth.

I have to say, I am honestly appalled at how the desire-rule paradigm of Genesis 3:16, which was a manifestation of *spiritual death*, is still a much-used model and touted as "God's design" for Christian homes today. It's time to live in *spiritual life* as fully redeemed men and women. This is key to re-engaging our call for fruitfulness, increase, and Kingdom dominion together in our God appointed territories. This is NOT to negate headship, but rather there is a true headship that God desires us to understand. We will look at this important dynamic next.

God wants His daughters to prosper. He does not want us to be manipulative or silenced. We have a voice and we must use it—appropriately, righteously, confidently, and respectfully, submitting our tongue to the Holy Spirit. And not only our tongue, but our whole life and heart from which flow the issues of life. Such submission is the path of true empowerment.

- 8 -

THE REIGN OF TRADITION

*"What we think, and what is true, are not always
the same thing."*

— J. Nicole Williamson

God has a course for each of us to run — a work to do, a purpose to accomplish. But sometimes, traditional mindsets keep us from running our race with courage and freedom as God intends.

Isaiah 62:10 talks of when God's people came out of captivity in returning to their divine place of purpose. The roadway back was laced with stones — things that would trip them up and cause them to stumble, or even fall. These needed to be removed.

Traditions are a set of repeated practices that can sometimes be like stones impeding our walk. When a tradition has been around for a long time, it becomes a norm. We do it because we've always done it…even if our practice causes another's pain.

The last point in question that I want to clarify regarding a woman's identity in marriage is the traditional mindset of headship. Paul not only had to correct women in how they treated their husband, but husbands in how they treated their wife. Paul battled many areas of traditional thinking as he advanced the Kingdom of heaven. He confronted mindsets that were like stumbling stones needing to be removed if the people were to come fully out of captivity and into a redeemed inheritance.

When the Lord began showing me the truth about headship, tears streamed. Not in anguish, but as overcome with glory! How could we have gotten this so wrong? In Christendom, we still so often think in fallen ways, even about divine truths. Isaiah 55:9 shows us that *His ways are higher than ours, and His thoughts than our thoughts.* How true it is.

The concept of headship is one that is far-reaching, not only for us as women, but also for the whole Church in understanding our identity as a cherished Bride of power.

Yet these two words, *Bride* and *power*, are typically not spoken together! They conjure up a *Jezebel* image. But we must understand that Christ's Body is *a Bride of power by the Holy Spirit*; Jezebel was a powerful queen of a wrong spirit, a demonic spirit. There is a vast difference...each one advancing a very different kingdom.

In the pages ahead, I will unfold what God says about true headship, as well as what it is not. But first, we must see another journey—the journey of Christ's own Bride that she has taken through the annals of religious history. There, we will see her encounter with Gnostic traditions that invaded Church culture. These philosophies altered the truth about the Church's own headship, and brought into Christendom the suppression of women. It laid another foundation other than Christ.

Again, we must understand that doctrines impacting women also impact the entire functioning of the Body of Christ. We must know the truth for us as women, but also for the entire Body of

Christ so that we rise confidently and gloriously for Kingdom living and cultural impact.

True headship is one of the most empowering dynamics in marriage and in the family of God. And yet, the inversion of it creates the opposite: dysfunction and disempowerment. Christ's own Beloved, made of men and women, often isn't so different than *Ishshah* in the garden. We listen to the deceptive whispering of *Abbadon*, and eat from the tree of the knowledge of good and evil rather than the tree of life.

Satan hates our prospering in divine purpose, and his greatest weapons have always been twisted perspectives, earthly thinking, and limited mindsets.

We've seen how women in the early Church blossomed under the apostle's boldness to follow God's design, overcoming cultural mindsets as they advanced the Kingdom of God on earth. However, as the early church leaders died the churches became vulnerable to the continued infiltration of cultural traditions and philosophies...with the latest being, *Gnosticism*. This philosophy viewed the body and femininity itself as inherently evil.

The influence of these fallen mindsets have shaped false ideologies of headship within the Church, and thus propagated not only a disempowerment of godly women, but also of the Church herself as a Bride.

Let's look.

SHIFTING CHURCH CULTURE

Until the fourth century, the early Church suffered much persecution, including tortures, burning, mutilations, starvation, and even martyrdom. Many had been condemned to killings in Rome's Coliseum—both men and women alike. Nero himself burned Christians as living torches for his evening parties. In 313 A.D., the Roman Emperor, Constantine, stopped the onslaught

147

and granted freedom of religion. No doubt, this was in favor of his own mother, Helen, who had converted to Christianity. Helen, formerly the wife of Emperor Constantius (Constantine's father), had been removed from influence in Rome's imperial court after their divorce. She later returned to the public life in 312 A.D., a few years after Constantine's rise to power (after his father's death).

Through the famous *Edict of Milan*, Constantine shifted Rome's culture by legalizing Christian worship. The emperor not only became a patron of the church (though not necessarily born again at the time), but also set a precedent of his own position of leadership within the Church itself.

Taking on a personal role of input, Constantine worked to resolve issues within the clergy by convening councils of bishops to define an orthodox (or "correct") Christian faith, *expanding* on earlier Christian councils. This led to the politicizing of the clergy because of Constantine's *organizational interest* to see the Church *and* the Empire prosper.[1]

With the Church united to Rome's power, *Rome's laws* such as "a woman is not allowed to hold any civil or public office," and that "a woman cannot be a valid witness, tutor or curator" were adopted into the Church and observed clear into the twentieth century in the West.[2]

The institution of the Church allowed Gnostic doctrines and Greek mindsets to mix with doctrines of faith. Once again, Christian women found themselves repressed rather than laboring as co-heirs in advancing the Father's Kingdom.

A few years later in 380 A.D., Emperor Theodosius I took the tolerance of Christianity a giant step somewhere (not forward) and made Nicene Christianity the Empire's sole authorized religion through the *Edict of Thessalonica*. The Church became an *official institution with political ties, and the state church of the Roman Empire* was born.

Greco-Roman style leadership with hierarchal order replaced the Church's five-fold leadership paradigm that had mentored intimate relationship with God through the power of the Spirit...the model established by Christ, the Church's true Head. *Religious structures replaced a Church of power.* Titles of sainthood were relegated to a chosen few with statutes erected in their honor, while God's people (who He calls saints) received new *customary ways* to try and gain favor with God through works. The reign of new traditions replaced true Kingdom advancement as a politically elected official took the seat as head of the Church.

This marked a new era, not just for Christian women, but also for Christ's Bride of all ages, race, and gender. While free from persecution, the Church now had an altered paradigm, a twisted model. And in it, she lost her true identity.

THE JOURNEY OF THE BRIDES

It's one thing to honor the government of heaven as we govern in the courts of earth, but it's another to insert worldly designs into the governing of Christ's Body. I call this era *the journey of the brides*, because you can't separate how women are viewed and treated from how the true Church is viewed and trained in her own identity.

From the beginning of this book I have endeavored to show how the journey of women and the journey of Christ's Bride are parallel. When the Lord began to speak to me about a woman's identity, He said, "Where we embrace a disempowered natural bride, we will embrace the concept of a disempowered spiritual Bride."

The Church itself is a governing Body as the Bride of the Ruler. Ruling territory is in our DNA as His Body. However, what the *politicizing* of the Church did was establish a counterfeit model to true Church headship and leadership, thus disempowering the Body. In the Church's new institutional order, a political government *controlled the Church*, seizing the power of its influence to strengthen an empire. In this structure, the apostolic movement was said to cease, the prophetic voice was decried to be a thing of the past, and spiritual gifts were denounced as dead or demonic...and the move of the Holy Spirit was quenched. The holy Bride became subjugated and silenced.

Added to this, the Church severed her connection with (then scattered) Israel. Replacement theology redefined the Church, removing the truth that we are grafted into God's new and bridal covenant with Israel in Christ. It was another blow to the Church's true identity (Jer. 31:31; Heb. 8:13). *Abaddon* was still at work.

Centuries later, this perverted control led to the religious atrocities we know as the Crusades...all done in the name of Christ! Nothing could be further from His nature or design. Misguided people of faith took up natural swords against human beings as the fervor of politicized religion burned with fleshly methods.

This was not unlike other movements the world has seen, including the Spanish Inquisition, Hitler's Nazi Germany, and even modern day radical Islam. These, all done in the name of "God," were and are not of God (*Yahweh Elohim, Creator*)!

The Father's Kingdom in Christ is a dominion of love and honor, not killing. His purpose is for a society's wholeness, not its destruction.

In spite of such a deadly blow to the Church's true identity and calling, great men of faith rose up through the centuries to keep the light of the gospel alive. However, even among these beloved reformers and renowned fathers of faith, some kept to *traditional* and Gnostic views of women.

Theologians across Europe in the Middle Ages, such as Gratian, Durandus, Scotus, and Ambrosiaster promoted views akin to some of the classical Greek thinkers and Talmud teachers such as: "women have no human intelligence" and "females are born as abnormalities."[3] Others also declared things like: "women are not human (except Mary, mother of Jesus), and **are not made in the image of God,** they **cannot receive authority from God**...only man can receive authority from God...men seeking to be holy **should not converse with women**...Christ said that **women cannot be saved**...**women do not rise** on the last day and when a woman dies she returns to nothingness." They touted such ideas that "scripture reserves baptism for men only...that **women have to wear veils because they are unclean,"** and that "**women are not capable of full human speech and are forbidden to speak in church."** [4]

And this is why we join Jesus and pray, "Father, forgive them, they know not what they do!"

THE UNION OF GNOSTICISM AND CHURCH DOCTRINE

Esteemed and influential Church leaders such as Tertullian, Martin Luther, Ambrose, St. Anthony, and St. Jerome all held views reflecting extreme gender bias. Their views still influence the Church today. A few quotes from their works include (emphasis mine):

- Tertullian (called "the father of Latin Christianity and founder of Western theology") wrote in his 'De Cultu Feminarum,' section I.I, part 2 (translated by C.W. Marx): "**Do you not know that you are Eve? The judgment of God upon this sex lives on in this age; therefore, necessarily the guilt should live on also.** You are the gateway of the devil; you are the one who unseals the curse of that tree, and you are the first one to turn your back on the divine law; you are the one who persuaded him whom the devil was not capable of corrupting; you easily destroyed the image of God, Adam. **Because of what you deserve, that is, death, even the Son of God had to die."**[5]

151

- "Woman is Satan's pathway to a man's heart. Woman pushes man to the 'Cursed Tree.' Woman violates God's laws and distorts his [man's] picture." — Saint Tertullian[6]

- [For women] "the very consciousness of their own nature must evoke feelings of shame." — Saint Clement of Alexandria, Christian theologian (c150-215) Pedagogues II, 33, 2 [7]

- "Woman was merely man's helpmate, a function which pertains to her alone. She is not the image of God but as far as man is concerned, he is by himself the image of God." - Saint Augustine, Bishop of Hippo Regius (354-430) [8]

- "Woman is the gate of the devil, the path of wickedness, the sting of the serpent, in a word a perilous object." — St. Jerome, 4th Century priest, theologian, historian[9]

- "Woman is a daughter of falsehood, a sentinel of Hell, the enemy of peace, through her Adam lost Paradise." — St. John Damascene, 8th Century bishop[10]

- "Woman was created to be man's helpmeet, but her unique role is in conception…since for other purposes men would be better assisted by other men." — Thomas Aquinas, 13th Century theologian[11]

- "Woman is the fountain of the arm of the devil. Her voice is the hissing of the serpent." — St. Anthony, 13th Century priest[12]

- "Women are on earth to bear children. If they die in *childbearing*, it matters not; that is all they are here to do" (works 20.84)…"The word and works of God is quite clear, that women were made either to be wives or prostitutes" (works 12.94). — Martin Luther, 16th Century monk and reformer[13]

- "Women are of themselves prone enough to take the ascendant over men, without need of giving them that of learning, which, puffing up the mind, would render them more proud and insupportable than before; the good opinion they would have of themselves, being inconsistent with the obedience to which they are bound."
  — Theophraste Renaudot Conference, 17th Century [14]

- From a book called *The Gospel of Thomas* (non-canonical, thought to originate within a school of early Gnostic Christians, origin may have been Syria):[15] *"Simon Peter said to them: Let Mary go forth from among us, for women are not worthy of the life. Jesus said: Behold, I shall lead her, that I may make her male, in order that she also may become a living spirit like you males. For every woman who makes herself male shall enter into the kingdom of heaven"* (Thomas-114). This saying reflected the low view of women in the Gnostic philosophy.[16]

These leaders are worthy of honor as they held high the flame of faith in God like a beacon through many a dark era, but their traditions kept women in darkness, repressed, and ineffective in their *full* God-given calling. They were fathers who failed to fully raise the daughters of God.

Embracing the concept of women made in the image of God meant women had restored spiritual authority and dominion together with men. And for many, that didn't fit the "command to rule over her" paradigm. Some today still hold to that same ideology.

Even recently, we've seen on a global platform the limiting of godly women: On July 29, 2013, Pope Francis affirmed, "But with regards to the ordination of women, the Church has spoken and says 'no'. That door is closed." He said this referring to a document by the late pontiff stating, "...the ban was part of the infallible teaching of the Church."[17] **Notice that he didn't say the**

153

infallible teaching of the *Word*, but of the (institutionalized) *Church*!

Are you getting this? I show you these things not to malign leaders who fail us, **but to show you where current doctrines restricting women in God find their foundation**...and it's not in God's Word or what Christ demonstrated! Nor is it in the model of the early Church, **but in fallen mindsets and traditions of men.** These men were leaders of modern day theology with voices that continue to guide Church doctrine, and thus culture.

To show you how these ideas prevail in Church culture today, a few years ago I oversaw the women's Bible studies at my local church when a woman presented me with a book on *Family Order* she wanted to teach. When I saw the foundation was Genesis 3:16, I knew where it was going. As anticipated, it was laced with statements like: "*unconditional* submission to a husband...the O.T. *orders* a woman to call her husband '*lord*'...a wife is judged on how they obey their husband's *every whim*...'he shall rule over you' is part of woman's curse and still holds true today...and we are *called* to be secondary." It also went on to say, "a wife and mother working outside the home is a departure from divine order."

We have already discovered the truth about such statements so I won't belabor these points, except to reiterate that women are not "mandated to live under the judgment"...oh, my! And as for working outside the home, read Proverbs 31...though it must never be at the neglect of the husband and family.

I believe that in these last days there is going to be a return to the importance of the home, but not in a sense of being *kept* or restricted to home. It will be a revival of embracing the value of family relationships and the home as a house of life.

This mixing of faith with fallen systems has created dysfunction within the Church and within many Christian homes. We are now in a day of empowerment—it's time to walk in truth and not the whispers of *Abbadon*.

HEADSHIP NOT HIERARCHY

Because of the Fall, love, honor, and unity in relationships are often so foreign to our way of thinking. Powerless structures are often easier than dealing with the issues of our heart, our own ego, or personal agendas. They are easier than having an honest conversation and working things out together in a family, a ministry, or even a business. While we tend to focus on who has a "last say," the question should be: have all voices been heard? Respected? Honored? Are we walking in love?

Before the Fall, there was no *hierarchal order*. That didn't appear until chaos appeared. Prior, there was a unified honoring, just as the Godhead does. The question in relationship isn't so much, who is the boss? Rather, am I loving and honoring this person? In hierarchy, I don't have to listen to you...just do what I say. But that isn't Christ's model. It is, however, the model of an institution. We were created for relationship from the heart, not *institutional* life.

The Church, like a marriage, is not a hierarchal system, though that is how some see it. Rather, God designed it to be a unified movement energized and empowered through love and honor. This is what creates fruitfulness and full function.

It takes male and female to be fruitful for the family. Likewise, God's work in the earth needs the unity of His likeness in the home, in culture, and in the Church! It takes both to advance fruitfulness in Kingdom purposes for earth's healing. Jesus' work cannot be done without the unity of His *whole* body functioning at full capacity.

THE POWER OF FORGIVENESS

How then do we respond to those who hold tight to traditions over truth? I know of only one way: forgive them, pray for them, love them, know the truth, and live accordingly. We walk by the

155

Spirit and not the flesh. We don't have time for further captivity in bitterness. We do not pick up a fleshly sword. We do, however, pick up heaven's sword of truth to live as free and empowered sons and daughters of God.

Remember, the only thing that hinders us is what we believe. I have learned that I can't live my life according to someone else's opinion. I am a light-bearer. I will no longer hide my gifts and calling under my own, or someone else's, false doctrinal basket. Nevertheless, I will honor another's freewill to think what they want. Meanwhile, I have a work to do with the Last Adam and with the many sisters and brothers who receive me.

Gross darkness is covering the earth. We must shine brilliantly with the Light of God as redeemed women and as an empowered Bride: fully awakened, fully activated, and fully releasing a Kingdom of divine power. The day has come where we must rise above disempowering models and methods. It's time to be about our Father's business together, in His image. It's time to know the truth about these issues so that we all move fully into the purposes of God for our life, calling, and our territory!

It's time now to put away the things of this world and go on to maturity. Maturity can only come by intimate connection to Truth, and Truth is a Person...His name is Jesus, Yeshua. He will empower us as a fruitful Bride, cherished and sitting with Him, ruling forever. Yes, we women too will rise to eternal life at Christ's side as a fully redeemed creation...and we don't have to become a male to do so!

And now for some really good news...what scriptures says about true headship!

- 9 -

THE BATTLE FOR TRUTH

"The truth will set you free. But first, it will [tick] you off."
— *Gloria Steinem*

Truth is what not only frees us, but empowers us to live the life God intends. Today, we are seeing the veil lift as the Body of Christ is throwing off shackles of false doctrines to rise in the empowering love of Christ's headship. *Abbadon's* influence is being exposed as many ministries are learning to identify where institutionalized structures have held the brides captive—that being, women in general and the Church itself as a whole.

Apostles and prophets are returning to true leadership roles while spiritual gifts are being revived. There is a remnant rising who are shaking off the shackles of traditions, who embrace women as sisters in ministry, and who embrace Israel as she awakens from her own slumber to the love of Yeshua. **This remnant is a host who dare to counter cultural reasoning and bring it captive to the mind of Christ.** The Church is returning to her identity as sons in God's image, and as an empowered Bride. She is rising up as a daughter of troops!

As we continue, I want you to see how loved, celebrated, and cherished you are. God's concepts of you are ones of care and empowerment. Abba Father wants you to know that He is NOT holding a hammer over you, nor is Jesus. He does not treat you with force, but with love and unending kindness to make you flourish in every way. You are the apple of His eye and the desire of His heart. He is not punishing you because of past failures or holding you back because of your gender. You are freed from judgments and shame. Did you hear that? I want you to get this deep down in your spirit.

THE REAL MEANING OF HEADSHIP

Now before you think this is for "married only," it's not! This is one of the most important lessons of all regarding your identity as a woman in Christ, whether married or not. Paul beautifully revealed how a husband-wife relationship is meant to flourish through Christ's own model of head-body unity with *His* Church. If you are married, this will give you fresh perspective of your unity with your spouse, as well as your relationship with Jesus. If you are not married, it will also certainly give you wisdom for a daughter, niece or friend, as well as for yourself in intimacy with Christ.

As we step into the light of headship, we can only do this effectively as we first understand what "head" means. The meaning of "head" (Grk. *"Kephale"*) has been a point of great theological debate. To determine clarity we have to ask, what did "head" mean in that time and place, and what would Paul's hearers have understood with that term?

Remember, words can change in meaning through the years, have various meanings in different cultures, and even in different contexts. Understanding Paul's use of the word "head" is key to grasping our position in a natural marriage as well as our place with Christ.

> *"For the husband is the head of the wife,*
> *as Christ also is the head of the church."*
> *(Ephesians 5:22)*

Yes, here we are back at Ephesus. And again, we see Paul teaching new converts in a Greek culture, explaining divine concepts. According to Greek literature, ranging from Greek Classical to Greco-Roman era (the time in which the New Testament was written), **studies consistently agree that the common meaning of "head"** *(Kephale)* **meant: "source, head waters, spring, the head of an animal (including human)."**[1] Basic biology teaches that the head of a person serves for a very important purpose: *to empower the life of the body for full function.* It is from the head that an electrical current flows with life-giving impulse to every part of the body for its health and growth.

It was, however, the **Latin** meaning for head ("caput" — leader) that was most often used by later *theologians*, as Latin became the language of the scholars. Since English, Hebrew, and Latin all share the word "leader" and "authority" as a common metaphor for "head," *this* interpretation (not original Greek literature) became the standard translation for headship regarding New Testament passages in Bible commentaries and seminaries — *"even though this meaning was foreign to Greek culture."*

As one resource puts it: "Thus, the forces of tradition in a male-dominant culture, the identical metaphor in three languages, and a less than familiar understanding of the Greek language as a whole, could very easily lend theologians to assume that the metaphor of "leader" and "authority" for head must be appropriate for Greek as well."[2]

Many theologians for centuries have taught that traditional headship means "authority over." That interpretation has led to a range of behavior from caring leadership to extreme subjection.

159

Some men support their wives in a culture of love while others require a wife to ask his permission to go places and do things, getting his approval on every decision, and submitting to him no matter what.

If you do the research yourself, you will see how fiercely this battle for meaning rages in Christendom. And it is the misinterpretation of "head" that been the foundation to continue the judgment model and the desire-rule paradigm in Christian homes. The problem with even some current theologians' conclusions is that they are often based on standard texts and translations, rather than original texts with original meanings in the original language and culture.

One of the most used resources by theologians today is the Bauer-Arndt-Gingrich Greek-English Lexicon, which states the idea of "source" was never the correct interpretation, but it means "authority." The truth, however, is that "authority" was *added through faulty research* based on Walter Bauer's Greek-German Lexicon, rather than being a true interpretation from original Classical Greek literature.

Now look at this! In Colossians 2:8,19, Paul said: "See to it that no one takes you captive through philosophy and empty deception, according to the *tradition of men*, according to the elementary principles of the world, rather than according to Christ...and not *holding fast to the head, from whom the entire body, being supplied and held together by the joints and ligaments, grows with a growth which is from God"* (emphasis mine).

Did you read that? The head SUPPLYING AND HOLDING TOGETHER to EMPOWER GROWTH, which is FROM GOD! Hmm, sounds like "source" to me. However, this does not negate the realm of authority given to men (and women) in the home, which we will look at later.

Paul's reference to captivity through *"elementary principles"* referred to the **delusive speculations of Gentile cults and of**

160

Jewish theories that lead a person into error. The "philosophy and empty deception" were teachings presented as *superior to faith in Christ.* These were undermining the free flow of life energy between Head and Body, thus disempowering growth and function.

We can say that this same principle works equally in a marriage between a husband and wife (head-body unit): we must see to it that we are not imprisoned through worldly philosophies, cultural traditions, or deceptive reasoning that would hurt and suppress vibrant life in our intimacy and journey together as a couple!

Had Paul wanted to use the word *authority* as a picture for a husband's role toward his wife (as some Christian leaders will tell you), he would have used the word *authority* (Grk. "exousia"). But he didn't! Why? Because the only place where a form of "authority" (or rule) was ever used in regards to marriage was, guess where? The Fall...the curse paradigm! It was never used at creation or in the redeemed marriage model.

Paul understood that if he had used the word *authority*, it would not only have painted a false picture of Christ in "control" over a perhaps "silenced" Bride, but it would have perpetuated an already established cultural and religious mindset of male-superiority and female-inferiority at work in a fallen world. And he didn't want to do that! Remember, he had just established her role of cooperation and submission to a husband (countering any *female*-superiority notion), and now he is explaining the husband's role toward a wife, to counter male domination.

Paul wanted to paint the picture of an *empowering head* with an *empowered body*. He wanted to portray a bride launched into her full destiny through the loving, catalyst power of a godly *Yod*. This is the model for husbands in a restored marriage paradigm. This is the picture of Christ and His Bride!

According to Jesus, the "head" or "master" of a household is a *"goodman"* (Luke 22:11). This means that he, *as the owner of all*

161

that pertains to his house, has the charge for its care, wellbeing and prosperity. A man's care causes his household to prosper. And since Paul clarifies that Jesus is the head of a man's union with his wife, the man is not only accountable for her wellbeing, but empowered by Christ to *prosper* her! Remember the circle of empowerment from 1 Corinthians 11:3.

A LOVE EMPOWERED BODY

While the main emphasis in Church culture regarding marriage has often been the woman's submission, the great emphasis in scripture is the man's love! Let's see:

"Wives, be **subject** to your own husbands, as to the Lord. For the husband is the **head** of the wife, as Christ also is the *head of the church*, He Himself being the **Savior** of the **body**. But as the church is *subject* to Christ, so also the wives ought to be to their husbands in everything. Husbands, **love** your wives, just as Christ also loved the church and **gave Himself up for her**, so that He might **sanctify** her, having **cleansed** her by the washing of water with the **word**, that He might **present** to Himself the church **in all her glory**, having no spot or wrinkle or any such thing; but that she would be **holy and blameless.**

So husbands ought also to love their own wives as their own **bodies**. He who *loves his own wife* loves himself; for no one ever hated his own flesh, but **nourishes and cherishes** it, **just as Christ also does** the church, because we are members of His body. 'FOR THIS REASON A MAN SHALL LEAVE HIS FATHER AND MOTHER AND SHALL BE JOINED TO HIS WIFE, AND THE TWO SHALL BECOME ONE FLESH'" (Eph. 5:22-31).

Jesus here is the proto-type for husbands since He himself acts as a husband for His Church. And honestly, He has some pretty big shoes to fill! No wonder He puts Himself as the head of the man to empower him for the task we are about to witness. It's also why we need to give both Him and an earthly husband the respect they deserve, *cooperating* in a culture of honor.

Let's take a brief look at the way Jesus displays headship as a Husband.

A LOVE-EMPOWERED WOMAN:

"Husbands, love your wives, just as Christ also loved the church and gave Himself up for her..."

As we've discussed, empowerment in a head-body paradigm happens through unity. And through this unity, the head supplies the electrical impulse causing the body to grow and function. What is this energizing current in a covenant marriage? Love! A woman is empowered through a man's selfless love, just as Christ has empowered us through His sacrificial Love. That's why control, abuse, stubbornness or ego has no place in intimate relationship.

Love works to see another person flourish, just as Jesus does for us, having come to give us life abundantly (superior, remarkable, exceeding in quality and measure). Again, this was a new way of thinking for some men.

As a husband, Jesus' love is never ego-driven; it "doesn't seek its own" (1 Cor. 13:4-7). He knows that the absence of love shuts down motivation, creativity, and life in any relationship. Thus, as the head and source, Jesus' love is always fresh, deep, pure, and unceasing to inspire and energize life, wellbeing, and prospering.

He knows our personal love-language and so manifests His love for us in every way...through affirmation, gifts, service, His personal attention to us, and through the intimate touch of His abiding presence.

A PROTECTED AND PROSPEROUS WOMAN:

*"...For the husband is the **head** of the wife, as Christ also is the head of the church, He Himself being the **Savior** of the **body**..."*

The head is a protector and benefactor. A "*savior*" (Grk. "*soter*") referred to princes, kings, deities or, in general, men who conferred special benefits upon their country, or who act as a deliverer and protector of the land and its people. A husband is a princely protector who delivers his beloved from harm, and confers benefits for her wellbeing and prosperity.

A WASHED WOMAN:

"*...so that He might **sanctify** her, having **cleansed** her by the washing of water with the **word**...*"

Jesus not only gave Himself sacrificially to redeem us, but His voice washes away doubt, unbelief, fear, and wrong thinking. His words bring hope and give us fresh expectation of divine good. His speaking encourages us with truth. His graciousness (not anger) woos and draws our heart toward Him. As Romans 2:4 says, *His kindness leads us to repentance.* The very sound of Him is like water to our spirit man. In fact, Revelation 1:15 says that the voice of the Fiery One is like the sound of many waters.

Words carry power. They are an energy that releases what is beneficial, or even what is harmful. We've all experienced what it's like in a relationship to hurl words at one another that deplete life. But Jesus washes us with words that renew strength, even when He corrects us. His perspectives refresh our mind, will, and emotions with heaven's counsel and truth.

Jesus' words are life-giving water to the soul. Paul here is speaking specifically of the words proceeding from the head of a relationship. How important it was for these new converts to understand that *cultural and religious philosophy* that demeans women was not Christ's way toward the female gender, especially a spouse. Encouragement, rather than blame and belittlement, was the new standard!

I am so grateful that I have an earthly husband who, over three decades of marriage, has always spoken encouragement and kindness toward me. At times, when I've felt overwhelmed, discouraged, or even angry, he consistently has been there for me with words that renew with faith, hope, and love. As a prince benefactor, he sees from a different perspective and empowers me to see past places of disappointment and hurt. He has been a true "head" in our relationship. And because of that, my heart delights to cooperate respectfully with Him. His love is the well-spring of my desire to honor him.

There is a line of teaching today that takes this particular verse way out of context, instructing a husband that it is *his* responsibility to *make* his wife "holy." Rather than *being* the word of refreshing to her, the Word is used in legalistic ways to "wash away her defilement." In other words, extreme control and enforcing restrictions on activities, involvements, and other personal engagements are used in order to "keep her pure." Remember, no one's purity comes from someone else's outward enforcements. Purity is an inward transformation through personal encounter with Christ and yielding our heart to the work of the Holy Spirit.

A WOMAN PRESENTED WITH GLORY:

*"...that He might **present** to Himself the church **in all her glory**, having no spot or wrinkle or any such thing..."*

Here we see a woman presented in all her glory. How very different from the "veil her and hide her in the house" ideology of Assyrian, Greek, or Talmud thinking. In Jesus' estimation, a bride is one to be celebrated! Jesus, as a Husband, does not make His Bride feel shamed, unwanted, unvalued, or worthless. He does not veil us, but does everything so that we shine in His goodness toward us...and everyone sees it, and loves Him for it! He's proud of His Bride!

Jesus adorns His Beloved with gifts and makes us the display of wisdom before principalities and rulers (Eph. 3:10). He *wants* us to radiate with the Spirit's abiding glory and His delight in us.

Again, this was contrary to the Babylonian Talmud and Greco-Roman mindset.

A CHERISHED WOMAN:

"...So husbands ought also to love their own wives as their own bodies. He who loves his own wife loves himself; for no one ever hated his own flesh, but nourishes and cherishes it, just as Christ also does the church..."

As the Head of His beloved, Jesus nourishes and cherishes us as His own body. Paul described the perspective of a head as seeing the body the same as himself—an extension of his own existence, not something separate. Thus, the body is something you certainly wouldn't abuse or shutdown. To do so would be hurting yourself. Therefore, the beloved is to be treated with nurturing care, cherished, provided for, and protected.

To *nurture* (Grk. *"ektrepho"*) means: to feed, cause to grow, nurture, and support. To *cherish* (Grk. *"thalpo"*) means: to keep warm, foster with tender care, and includes listening to another's needs and desires.

The Last Adam does not *demand* obedience of us as His beloved, or say things like, "You *have* to obey Me!" That's because His focus isn't Himself, but making us feel secure, respected, and beautiful as we grow in grace. And most of all, He does not hurt us or treat us harshly. He wants our yielding to Him to be the synergy of love, not a fearful response to an order.

Statistics show that one in four women (25%) will experience domestic violence in her lifetime[3]...and these numbers only reflect the physical abuse that is reported, not the verbal and emotional abuse that occurs. And what's more, such actions happen in Christian homes as often as in any other!

Unfortunately, as I said earlier, many of these women who seek pastoral help are often told to *submit* to their husband based on *biblical* principle, or are simply not believed, or even told that they "deserved it." Reports show that even some pastors are abusive in their own home, again using Genesis 3:16 to support their "right to rule" in such a way. [4]

This is the opposite of Christ's headship who loves, protects and cherishes His Bride. Do you see where some of what we are taught in Christendom does not come from Christ, but from another source…from fallen-laced traditions?

A WOMAN OF ABUNDANCE:

"And the church is his body; it is made full and complete by Christ, who fills all things everywhere with himself" (Eph. 1:23).

Paul portrays the bride as someone who is *made full and complete*. The Greek word for *"complete"* (Grk. "pleroma") is the picture of a ship that is filled with supplies and manned with workers and military presence. In other words, our identity as the beloved is as a ship filled with an abundance of goods wherever we go, bringing benefit and military assistance! Nothing lacking.

I cannot emphasize this enough that God's view of a woman and bride is esteemed so very high!

CULTURE OF HONOR

Marriages and relationships today are in crisis and they need divine love and truth for full healing. We have just seen how Christ, as a Heavenly Husband, relates to and treats His Bride. **His model is the true biblical standard for marriage.**

Some, reading these words, may have experienced something quite different in an earthly marriage. But in God's goodness towards us, part of the *goods* we carry as a woman of abundance is the healing balm of God's love to be infused into every wound and dark memory. He has given us the Spirit of deliverance from rejection, self-hatred, and judgments that we have internalized. Wholeness comes as we wash in the pool of Jesus' intimate love and affirmation. We have front row seating with Him to soak in the healing rays of His Light that breaks the spell of *Abbadon's* evil and destructive whispering.

Headship by Christ's model is not one of superiority, arrogance, force or abuse. Rather, His leadership is one of servanthood that causes us to be confident in His love, and thus prosperous. In fact, in God's paradigm for headship, the place of supreme honor is given to the one who lays down his life and builds up his family. *Jesus was given the place of preeminence because of His humble sacrifice – not because of His right to dominate.* It is His loving sacrifice that captures our affections and moves our heart to honor Him.

Jesus is not a controller, but He is accountable and responsible for His household. In that responsibility, He gives us freewill AND authority—raising us up to sit with Him at His side, together with Him on His throne. Yes, I said authority, which we will look at next.

Loved and valued is your identity as a woman. Don't let anyone else tell you any different. You are esteemed in the eyes of the Heavenly Lover of your soul. You are His queen. Believe it. Walk in it. And know that His eyes beam brilliantly as He presents you proudly.

- 10 -

WOMEN WITH AUTHORITY

*"The most common way people give up their power is
by thinking they don't have any."*

— Alice Walker

The longer I walk with Jesus, the more I experience the
beautiful reality of my emancipation from the Fall and its
penalty. It seems I encounter new areas of restoration in
being a woman of God's image every day, making life's journey
inexplicably wonderful. Included in these redeemed realms is the
seat of authority I am given in Christ.

Yes, even women have restored authority. What? Blasphemy!
Unfortunately, this is the response in some Christian circles. They
feel that *women* and *authority* are incongruent terms. However,
they are not.

Because of my upbringing, I too saw women and authority as
polar terms, like words not to be mentioned in the same
sentence...God forbid...at home, or in the Church.

As a young mother, I knew my place was important in raising our children, but Christian influences impressed me that when my kids became teens I was to take my hands off and leave the "managing of the children" to the head of the home, my husband. Since he was the authority, he could better handle young adult instruction. In other words, mothers were for small children, fathers were for raising young adults.

Talk about gullible.

By the time our kids were well into their teens and going through the challenges of those transitional years (what did we call it earlier? Ah yes, "sprouting horns"), I felt I'd lost all authority in my own home. And I had...I had given it away through false teaching.

God meant for both the father and mother to raise the children together. Children were never instructed to listen to their mother ONLY until puberty. But more than one voice made it clear to me: I was to take a back seat. I was not the head, thus I had no "authority." This was more than simply giving space to our teen children to grow; it was robbing my voice to speak at all.

This concept of "teaching only the young" is the same philosophy that we so often see promoted in the institutional Church where women can be singers, Sunday School teachers and secretaries...but not leading adult training from a pulpit, and certainly not teaching men. I've heard countless firsthand stories, even current ones, both here and abroad, of men angered because a woman spoke from behind a pulpit.

Tradition has emphasized that the male is the leader and the female is the follower—always and everywhere in Christendom. As stated before, it is because of this view that some women are held back from leadership together with a spouse, or in ministry...unless you want to be a missionary, in a foreign country, just not here, where we can see and hear you.

Yet, even there women often find prohibitions.

This view of women without authority is rooted in the faulty understanding of headship that we just addressed, a place where only a man has authority. Because of this, many women shrink back in fear (and in respect for tradition) from the work that Christ has called and gifted them to do. The voice of spiritual mothers is neglected, silenced, and with it, the authority designed to govern territory for its wellbeing.

Let's look at what scripture says on this subject.

CLARIFYING AUTHORITY

For clarification, a man is the head of his home AND has authority over the home. See, I didn't take his authority away. However, though the woman is not the head, she too has authority. Yes, gasp and faint.

First of all, I want you to see that the word "authority" comes from the word "author" which means: one who brings something into being, initiator, one who *fathers* a thing. From this we understand that the nature of authority is, foremost, relational for the purpose of prospering a thing. Authority is designed to operate in a fathering way. And no wonder, since all authority comes from God, and God is a Father—THE Father.

Second, what is authored or fathered is the fruit of unity. In a marriage, the man initiates a life, but the woman actually *develops and brings forth* the life. The fruit of their union results in a new life in their territory called family. **Remember, authority, as you will see, is for the wellbeing of life within territory.**

Since both male and female are involved in ruling territory, both are needed to "father" and "mother" (parent) the life within its boundaries for prospering.

Now, we've already seen the unity of the head-body paradigm in which the husband is identified as the head to empower the woman as the "body" for energized movement and prosperity in divine purpose. But now we see another dynamic where authority comes in to play, and in Jesus' model of the head-body paradigm, authority is shared. And what's more, it is a deliberate act on the part of the man to share the authority with his bride over their mutual territory! Remember, Adam was the first to be given the command to rule, but as God saw them as one, she too was given ruling authority.

Let me explain.

When a man, as an authority-carrying catalyst and divine *point-man* as a *spark* for God's purposes, takes a wife into covenant, the two become one. She too is a carrier of covenant and receives his authority for the territory they share, since they are one. This is what Jesus does for us as His beloved. Jesus has all authority and in our unity with Him He says, "I give you authority!" (Luke 10:19)

This is so important for us to get for our life and purpose on earth! When we become one with Christ, He gives us His authority for our home called earth. A Bride without authority is a powerless, disempowered Bride...which we are not!

For a man to not give a spouse authority is contrary to Christ's model. But look at this: since women (under Greek philosophy and Gnostic doctrines) were not held in unity with a husband (as her being human was even questioned), and since she was thought to be prohibited entrance into heaven, you can see why authority was not something to be given her!

This validated their thinking that only a man had authority. For him to give her authority meant the man had to see her as himself, which he did not. Yet unity and duo authority is how it was at the beginning...when *Iysh* saw *Ishshsah* as himself!

This is such a critical revelation! In our relationship with Jesus, He sees us as Himself, that's why He gives us authority. A body without authority has no functioning power against the works of darkness. This is why unity and authority in a head-body paradigm is foundational for understanding how we are to operate in the Kingdom, in the home, and in the Church...or perhaps better put, AS the Church!

REALMS OF AUTHORITY

So far, we have clarified the nature of authority as being relational for the prospering of life, and that in a home setting it is not about a man *subduing* his wife, rather, he gives her authority for prospering their territory together. **It was the Fall that created a one-sided and fallen rulership.**

Let's look further at what scripture says about authority and why it's given.

The Greek word for *authority* (*"exousia"*) means: *judicial power and rule of government, what is lawful with liberty to do and exercise power.* God established judicial authority as the right and power to protect, govern, and prosper *with justice* what He gives us to *bring forth.* We have authority from the courts of heaven to prosper what is under our care, protecting its wellbeing as we labor to lift up what has been brought forth into divine destiny.

We begin by exercising authority over darkness in our personal life to cut off destructive influences. We purposefully unite with the Holy Spirit in the authority given us for heaven's designs on earth. The courts of earth too were established by God to uphold justice *in accordance with heaven's designs*, and not to do as they please.

New Testament scriptures deal specifically with two kinds of authority: *civil* (what governs land and its inhabitants) and *spiritual* (what governs spiritual dimensions whether good or evil, including earth's elements since matter came from the unseen realm—Heb. 11:3).

Civil authority is the judicial power of civil rulers and government to *protect* people and interests within a territory from enemy invasion and wrongdoers. Whatever offends or opposes life and wellbeing is apprehended, contained, or removed.

A civil authority has the right to enforce protection from violators, with weapons if need be. It has the right and power to let you in, see you out, and even incarcerate you.

This works wonderfully when the authority is just; it works destruction when it is corrupt.

Now let's look at spiritual authority.

SPIRITUAL AUTHORITY

The Apostle Paul wrote about rulers, principalities, thrones and dominions both in heaven and on earth, visible and invisible. He made it clear that all things have been created through Christ and for Him (Col. 1:16). He also said that God uses Christ's Body, the Church, to display His wisdom before spiritual rulers and authorities in heavenly places (Eph. 3:10).

It is there, in heavenly places with Christ who is at the right hand of the Father, that we too are seated (Eph.1:20; 2:6). When Jesus said, "I give you authority," it was a declaration for *all* who are born of His Spirit, and not just for a few men who lived a long time ago!

We must remember that nothing on earth involves merely natural dynamics, but spiritual as well since all things seen came from what is not seen.

The Last Adam is the Ruler of Nations and He gives His Body spiritual authority for spiritual dominion in the territory where He places us — territory that is both spiritual and natural.

As Christ's Bride, we have spiritual authority to *rule with judicial spiritual power over territory.* This right and power is to protect territory against the works of darkness while promoting liberty and the prosperity of life under Christ's government.

In Christ, our spiritual authority (exousia) is described as being:

- Over unclean spirits and all demons - Matt. 10:1; Mark 6:7; Luke 9:1
- To heal all disease - Luke 9:1
- To govern cities - Luke 19:17
- To tread serpents and scorpions (demon powers) - Luke 10:19
- Over the nations – Rev. 2:26
- Over the elements – Matt. 8:26

The purpose of spiritual authority is given to advance the Kingdom of heaven on earth. It manifests as healing, deliverance, and breaking spiritual strongholds which hold people, cities, and nations in bondage. Spiritual authority releases prosperity of life and wellbeing for growth and movement with God's design. **It is a judicial power from the courts of heaven over darkness.**

Notice that none of the scriptures we've just seen portray a man as having "authority" over his wife. The only use of the word authority used in any marital context pertains to both the husband *and* wife in *NOT* exercising authority (*exousia*) as a judicial command regarding intimacy. They are not to withhold intimacy from one another, except for times of praying and fasting. Otherwise, a man and wife are to seek to *please the other person.* In other words, sex is not to be used as a tool of manipulation nor a personal right. Neither is it to be used for *forced* self-gratification (1 Cor. 7:4, 33-34).

A husband and wife are one. They belong to one another. *Exousia* is what we exercise **over our own body, not another's**...not even our spouse.

Let me put it this way: *Exousia* **is how Jesus relates to all things created — both visible and invisible;** *Agape* **(divine love) is how He relates to His Bride!**

175

Likewise, exousia is how we relate to territory, but Agape love is how a husband is to relate to a wife. He is not to *"exousia over her,"* rather he is to love her and *"proestemi"* over his household (*manage as a protector-guardian*, 1 Tim.3:4-5). This was foundational understanding for anyone desiring leadership in the Church in Paul's day—a position NOT of exousia over God's people, but of *"epimeleomai"* meaning: to care for with forethought and provision, as what the good Samaritan did.

So if Jesus gives His Bride authority for her home (the earth), then why are we taught that a natural woman has no authority? And worse, that she must submit to oppression or abuse since it's "a man's right according to scripture!" But it isn't. Jesus does not use His authority against His own Body to harm us at will. That's why Paul even used the example that a man doesn't hurt his own body, but nourishes it…neither should a man hurt his wife, but nurture her (Eph. 5:29).

It takes humility to share authority and care for another without dominating them. It takes humility to protect and guard them without imprisoning them. It takes humility to provide leadership without negating the leadership of the other one. It also takes humility to control your tongue and honor another person in the midst of differences. And when this happens, when the two walk in unity, humility, and authority…watch out world! Here comes the display of power and wisdom before the principalities and powers of darkness!

FOR THE LOVE OF THE HOME

In Christendom, the arguments regarding authority rage on every side. No doubt, everyone has one main objective: the valued sanctity of the home. I recently read an article that stated: "If you ever meet an egalitarian claiming that the word "head" in the Bible doesn't mean "authority" but means "source," you may wonder how to answer. Their purpose, of course, is to get rid of the idea of authority in the family."[1]

First, we NEED authority in the home.

Second, the issue is not about removing authority, but understanding what it is and how it operates. Only when our hands are free from a false paradigm can we pick up the true authority that God has given us. Perhaps if we were more concerned about exercising our authority against the works of darkness, we wouldn't be so concerned about trying to hurl "authority" at each other!

Even some women hold tight to traditional fallen views of women in the home and in the Church. Recently, I read an online article, (written by a woman) titled *"Feminism: The Caustic Explosion That is Destroying America."*[1] Since I'm an advocate for the wellbeing of our nation, the title caught my attention. Here's an excerpt from the article:

"Since feminism was mottled together out of a deep disdain for God's perfectly created order for men and women, it fueled the desire to rebel against the foundations of family. Therefore, the erosive movement was able to gain intense momentum as it was paired perfectly with a societal shift. Our nation became less concerned with foundations, more influenced by European Marxism, and sought out the Babylonian cry for feminism among women, and later brought along men, who all reject God. Suddenly, the use of the once sacred mortar of our foundations of God, Constitution and iron-clad families of strength, were abandoned to pursue anti-godly endeavors and selfishly built altars of sin. It was inevitable by this point, that this movement would begin the most corrosive of all forces to weaken the fortress of family, and bring down the entire societal house of cards; from the inside out."

Now, I haven't researched the foundation for her words, nor do I claim any tie or support of feminism. Honestly I'm too busy advancing my Father's Kingdom to know exactly what they do. But it just seems to me that the author of this article assumes the motive of *all* involved to be a God-hating rebellion with a desire to destroy family. But maybe, just maybe, a feminist's push for freedom isn't a rebellion against *GOD's* true design for family, but against the deep wounding women often experience from man-made traditions. Maybe they are looking to feel valued, loved, and cherished, but what they've experienced has been quite the opposite. It's just a thought.

It's easy to hurl names like "feminist" and how they are "home destroyers," but have we ever stopped to hold an honest conversation to discover the real issue? The heart issue? Are we hearing their true cry? Or do we just want them to obey the rules and sit down and be quiet. After all, it's what women are supposed to do.

In Western culture, I believe we have had a knee-jerk reaction about a woman's place. "Keeping a woman bare-foot and pregnant" used to be a standard joke, yet was also founded in a cultural mindset. Now, with the advent of women's rights, maternity clothes have often been exchanged for career attire. The pendulum has swung the other way, and it is this fear that some have regarding the feminist movement. But to suppress them isn't the answer either.

Fear of a woman's freedom was one of the great factors holding back granting a woman's right to vote until the 1920's. It was "opposed by many Christian leaders because of fear that a woman's attention [would be] diverted from her domestic duties, and thus a collapse in the family structure." [2]

Paul supported the importance of women being keepers of the home, though not "kept AT home" (as was taught in Talmud). The ministry of the home, family, and hospitality is not only highly esteemed by God as part of His likeness and nature, but is a critical building block for a healthy society. It must not be negated, yet not made to be a prison either.

Marriage was never intended to be a realm of repression, but for a man and woman to walk through life together in love.

Unfortunately, in our culture today, we see motherhood so often downplayed. However, children are a heritage! When I was a young stay-at-home mom, I often got pitiful looks from other women when asking what kind of work I did. Seriously. It got to the point that I felt embarrassed to say I was a stay-at-home mom! It was as if I wasn't smart or ambitious enough to have a career. It was worse when I said I was a home-schooling mom! Oh the looks. But I wouldn't have traded those precious years with my children for anything in the world.

Many mothers today don't have a choice and must work outside the home. I'm grateful for the opportunity I had.

AUTHORITY IN THE CHURCH

Now concerning the Church, there are appointed overseers (elders) to *care for* Christ's Body. These have not been given *judicial power* over Christ's Body, but are given to care for their maturing in Christ for doing the work of ministry through the equipping of the apostles, prophets, evangelists, pastors, and teachers. Nevertheless, from the time of Constantine (as we discussed previously), it was the *institutional Church* that promoted a hierarchal structure of *authority*, not just in the family, but in the family of God. This structure established a chain of command (emphasis on command, and control) in a place God never intended.

I remember being in one church for a time where I can't count how many times we were told we "must obey" whatever the pastor said or we would be swallowed like Korah for rebellion against authority. "Touch not mine anointed" (referring to the pastor as the *anointed one*) was well engrained in us, lest we be smitten by God for disobeying His *delegated authority*. Sadly, I remember one nine-year-old boy who was made to stand and be humiliated in front of the congregation for "lack of faith" that God could heal him. We were also constantly reminded that God was "scrutinizing" us in how we gave our offerings. I'm not kidding.

179

And this is more common than not. Spiritual abuse, like domestic abuse, is rampant.

I remember other events, too, like when I was eighteen and attending a church retreat (this was a different church). I brushed past a church leader who didn't like my attitude. He grabbed my neck, dragged me to another room, and threw me down. Then with fist held high, threatened to beat me if I didn't straighten up. Another time (years later in a different church), I had just lost our first child in a miscarriage. By then I had been walking closely to the Lord for several years, but the pastor told me that God took my baby as punishment for how rebellious I had been as a youth.

I remember these incidents now with pity for them. I am not a victim; I am more than an overcomer. I may have been a mouthy teen, but authority was never intended to abuse — physically, verbally, or spiritually. I do not accept the hammer-concept of authority, but I do accept my own responsibility to love and honor.

Christ's authority is never about controlling or subjecting people, especially His Bride! Subjugation means: to conquer and overcome through power. Christ's authority is about healing, restoring, and giving life. He is the *Author of salvation* — One who confers life-giving benefits! True authority lays its life down for another's wellbeing, not bonking them on the head with our scepter. There is no place for domineering in our dominion...not for men or women. Instead, we must hold the scepter against the enemy!

This is so important because where we embrace false authority in the home, we will easily embrace false authority in the church, and vice-versa. Not only has the headship paradigm been twisted, but also nowhere in Scripture does it say that apostles, prophets, evangelists, pastors or teachers have *exousia* over God's people. They have the *care for* (Grk. *"epimeleomai"*) God's people and exousia over the works of darkness. There is a difference. Nor are they the head of the Church...Jesus is.

Nevertheless, some have viewed their care as *exousia*, which has created misguided control in the Church. It is when false authority is exercised (in church and in the home) that we encounter abuse, oppression, and repression of the gifts and callings of God.

A BRIDE OF POWER

A friend told me one time of a conversation she had with a pastor who admitted that he understood his place as a son of God, but struggled with the concept of being called a "Bride" to Christ. I'm sure there are other men who have felt the same. Unfortunately, it is, no doubt, because of Christendom's often powerless portrayal of a woman's identity. I understand. But this is rooted in the wrong concept of a bride, as we have seen.

I pray for their understanding, meanwhile, we must display what it truly means to be an empowered Bride—confident, wise, and exercising the authority given us in Christ. We must rid ourselves of any filter in our thinking of being anything less than filled with divine abundance for Kingdom impact.

I believe that when the world begins to see women knowing who they are in Christ, the Church releasing women into their full destiny in Him and working in unity with brothers, the world will see a Church rise in unity and power. **As long as spiritual gifts are denied, divine healing is negated, apostles and prophets are relegated to a ceased era, and women are viewed as subordinate, the world will continue to see a powerless Church. And this list includes where the Church continues to refute her spiritual heritage with Israel through replacement theologies and anti-Semitism.**

The same holds true for marriages. When the world sees godly men lovingly release their bride into unsuppressed divine design, and a woman honoring her husband without being a doormat or devourer, we will see the display of God's name and blessing in accelerated increase in the home and culture. The truth is, when any of us (male or female) embrace a false ideology, responsibility, or even authority we disengage ourselves from doing the true will of our Father.

There will always be those who hold to particular *fallen* traditional views. Nevertheless, there is a remnant rising who refuse the limitations of man-made traditions for a life of fullness in Christ to heal nations with heaven's presence.

Satan's ploy is to get us entangled with a counterfeit that "feels" biblical, but robs us of His authority. We must stop drawing philosophy from the *curse paradigm*. The earth is languishing to see the sons and daughters of God rise in authentic leadership that empowers life rather than living under the curse of chaos that consumes through control.

Christ's authority is given to us to destroy chaos, not promote it! And the last I've seen, our homes and society are in dire need of chaos being destroyed. Interestingly, the Hebrew word *curse* ("*qalal*")"not only reflects a control that withers life, but it also means: *to treat another with no value.*

It's time to step into the power of full redemption and restored value! Let the *Ezer's* arise!

Christ's Bride is not an oppressed or subjugated Body. She is not a doormat or a devourer. She is not a captive. She is one with Christ, seated at His side, every part functioning in power. She is filled with good things to minister out of that fullness.

She heals the brokenhearted, casts out devils, raises the dead, opens blind eyes, works miracles, and equips the children of God to be fruitful in every way. She pioneers new frontiers, establishes good works, prophesies the word of the Lord, and disciples nations.

She is a game changer, culture shifter, nation healer, and Father pleaser who preaches the gospel, confidently! She develops and uses her gifts. She is the display of God's wisdom before rulers. She is not afraid, and most of all, she loves and honors. This is our identity in Christ for both men AND women!

So untraditional!

So let theologians debate our place and the philosophers formulate ideas about us. Meanwhile, we have a work to do with Christ. And He is calling us to rise with Him in authority, in this last hour, to care for our homes, communities, and the nations.

- 11 -

DAUGHTERS, ARISE!

*"The question isn't who's going to let me;
it's who is going to stop me!"*

– Ayn Rand

I have led you on a journey from creation and through the cultures until this moment in time. I hope you now see the brilliance of who you are as a woman, regardless of any difficulty you may have experienced in life. You are loved and you are triumphant in Him.

In fact, as we close, let's review all the beautiful things that Father has laced into your nature as a daughter in His likeness. You are a fiery leader, an overcomer, a completer, a revelator, communicator, and promoter of life. You are a reconciler, priestess, and intuitive helper. You are gifted to bring increase, with progress and completion, for the accomplishment of divine purpose. You are a house of life. You are a perceptive warrior and a weapon in God's hand for earth's wellbeing. You have divine timing intertwined in your movement.

You are a face-to-face counterpart who carries the maternal image of God. You are a gateway to life and wealth with the ability to bring breakthrough for another's life and destiny. You are the bearer of new life—a next generation of those also called to bear God's image, carry His glory, and walk in His purposes to make His presence known.

Your words, touch, influence, and leadership lifts others, and brings them great benefit. You are highly and delightfully affirmed in who you are. You are accepted. Celebrated! You are God's prophetic declaration of jubilee and manifest promise of redemption and return to inheritance. You are an access way between the seen and unseen, and a fully loaded ship of heaven's provision for your territory and purpose on earth.

You are cherished, loved, highly favored, seated in heavenly places with divine authority as the display of God's wisdom before rulers and principalities—on earth and in the heavens. You are an empowered woman as the Father's daughter.

Wow! No wonder *Abbadon* works with great enmity against women and against the entire Bride of Christ lest we rise into our full identity in Him.

THE RISE OF FIERY LEADERS

Now that we see how God has fashioned us to advance our Father's Kingdom on earth, we must let go of old ways of trying to find an identity through what we do, a position, career or ability we have, how we look, or through another person. It's time to stand strong, together with our brothers, for the healing of the nations. We have a work to do in every realm of culture as God leads us. This also means NOT picking up responsibilities that God does not give us, which we women are so often prone to do.

Remember, the Last Adam came declaring His identity—it wasn't a pride thing, rather it was *an agreement with God about His personhood and mission.* We've all recoiled when hearing someone's prideful tooting of their own horn; we've repented when we've done it ourselves. Nevertheless, too many have migrated to the opposite end of the stick of "humbly" denying their gifts and voice.

We applaud those in front, and urge others forward, all the while negating or neglecting what God is telling US to do. I know, so been there, done that. But something, especially of late, has taken hold of my spirit with urgency for this hour. I, for one, just don't have time for passivity or hesitation any more...and neither do you, sweet sister. We must rise and follow the leading of the Spirit and open our mouth! And if we're wrong, then we accept correction.

It's time to boldly reconcile our homes and culture to life.

This isn't about seeking fame or recognition before people, but about moving with Father's heart to advance His Kingdom. And since His passion is for the souls of mankind, then it must be our passion too in reconciling mankind to His love.

Christ is the manifest love of the Father. He is called the Desire of the Nations, because who else could possibly care for them like He does? No one.

As His face-to-face counterpart, we must take up our sword and dance with Him to loose the prisoners from darkness. We must stop hiding in the shadows and step into our identity as His leadership in union with Him.

Father wants us to know who we are in Christ, and say who we are as we rise up and boldly step into our appointed place of action...and not be ashamed! Not second-guess. Not cower and say, "I'm sorry. I can't. Who am I? I'm just a woman."

It is a day to be courageous and do exploits, to know His Name and carry His liberating presence into our sphere of influence. It's time to declare our agreement with God about our identity in Him and our mission.

187

THE RISE OF THE COMMUNICATORS

The world needs the burning ones who will rise with heaven's healing in their words and hands. We've learned from Paul, and the "Amazon" women of Ephesus, that being empowered is not about being masculine, arrogant, or self-willed. Recently my son told me of a woman who came into the store where he manages, spouting profanity and verbally abusing him as she aired her complaint. After he dealt with the situation, he noticed her drive off in a car with a license plate that read: EMPOWERED. That is not the kind of empowering we need!

As God is restoring the importance of the woman's voice in Christendom, Father wants our voice to carry His words and not the power of angry flesh as a way to be heard...or seductive flesh as a way to be seen. Too often women have felt that anger and seduction are the only ways to get the affirmation we need or recognition we desire. But it is not so.

As truly empowered women, if we look to God, we will see that He affirms us as He moves on our behalf in miraculous ways. We don't have to push and shove or do things the way the world does them. We are fashioned for a different purpose. We must move in a different way...the way Holy Spirit shows us as we cultivate intimacy with Him every day.

I've learned on my journey of the importance of cultivating a life-style of God's presence. Such a lifestyle is one of intimate prayer and worship that transforms me as I connect with the heart of God. It includes time in His Word as I engage with Holy Spirit to bring me understanding and revelation. These not only develop intimate relationship with God, but are great detoxifiers of the soul, too.

These give me new ability to see situations from God's perspective, to discern what is true and what is not true, and helps me to speak what He speaks...and be quiet when I need to be quiet! Intimacy with God gives me counsel and wisdom for right action. An empowered life as the Last Adam's counterpart means I must be strongly united to my Source...my beautiful Head, Jesus.

Words carry power and even in the smallest of conversations we have the ability to create heaven's environment on earth, lift others out of fear and despair, and promote joy. Precious woman, you are important! There are people, young and old, who need you. They need your voice in harmony with Holy Spirit. The Word of God in you is powerful as a two-edged sword to open blind eyes, heal broken hearts, and set captives free. There's authority in your mouth! People are waiting to hear His life-giving words through you! Open your mouth and let God fill it.

THE RISE OF THE TRUTH BEARERS

True empowerment in our Father's likeness requires us to remove every vestige of fear, false doctrines, and *false* humility (as well as pride) that has infiltrated our belief system. To live as an empowered Bride of the Ruler of the Nations, we must step out of old structures we once trusted in, but limited our fruitfulness...even to the shutting out of the Kingdom of heaven (such as what we've discussed throughout these pages).

I have become keenly aware of how much cultural influences have tainted my own understanding of biblical truths. That's why I'm clarifying truths in these pages because Truth sets us free for divine destiny. Truth is the power that energizes our intimate movement with God. No truth means no power. Truth filtered through the dirty lens of wrong beliefs means short-circuited power.

Why did Jesus move in unlimited power and authority? Because He came as pure, undefiled, Truth. His thoughts were free from Greco-Roman views, Talmud twists, and religious restraints. He was free! He thought as His Father thought...thus He rules. He was never a victim, not even on the cross.

189

This morning, I woke up early with an old song we used to sing resonating in my spirit. The words are from Revelation 22 and it goes like this: *And He showed me a pure river of the waters of life, clear as crystal proceeding out from the throne of God. And in the midst of it, and on either side of the river was the tree of life.* And this is what the Lord spoke to me: "My truth is living water that is crystal clear, pure, undefiled. My truth is life-giving power."

Sometimes we think it's our faith that fails us, but more often it is the tainted forms of truth we embrace that is the source of disempowerment in our lives. I love how the Bible ends with the Holy Spirit and Christ's Bride calling out in unison for people to come and drink of these waters that flow with divine authority (Rev. 22). God wants His image in us empowered with His Truth!

Christ's Bride knows that her power comes from the crystal waters of God's Truth that governs all things seen and unseen. His truth is like a crystal glass that rings with a pure tone, as opposed to a glass of philosophy that carries no sound of life, at all.

Revelation from God is all around us. Can we hear it? Do we see it? Maybe we need to check what glass we are drinking from, or how pure the water is that we are internalizing. Remember, Jesus' Bride is a washed Bride—she's a swimming champ in the waters of life and she drinks from a crystal glass!

THE RISE OF ROYAL INTERCESSORS

The life of God in us is for the healing of nations. Healing nations requires the *whole* body of Christ to rise in every place of society—and not just a few men out front. The Holy Spirit today is moving to bring a new unity between men and women to parent not just their children, but cultures and mountains of society.

Nations around the world are in critical states of change, needing wisdom from above and the words of those who will speak it boldly. Nations are desperate for those who will intercede on the behalf of their social wellbeing. As the Apostle John stated, we are spiritual kings of territory and priests of reconciliation, just as it was in the beginning (Rev. 1:6).

We have access to the throne of God to carry our family, community, and nation to Him in prayer as we speak with Him on everything that concerns them. We are seated with Christ in heavenly places with open access to hear heaven's decrees and speak on earth what we hear in heaven. His decrees in our mouth carry power.

We have the ability to shift culture through intercession and decisive actions as He leads us.

On our journey over the past few chapters, we have seen how the written codes and edicts of kings and emperors have shifted the culture of entire nations. Just today I read an article of how Russia's leader, Stalin, less than a century ago, took deliberate government action to eliminate the celebration of Christmas in his country. The holiday was replaced with a Winter Festival, portrayed with different characters, and celebrated on a different day—New Years.[1]

One stroke of a royal pen changed a nation.

But here it is: we have royal pens too! As we get into God's presence and hear His decrees we write them, pray them, and declare them. And too, His Word is full of His decrees that we can declare as He highlights what He is saying for specific situations.

At the time of this writing, America is experiencing huge shifts in culture through edicts from our own government, especially regarding America's founding values. Even the gay agenda is not simply about one's sexual preference; it is a crafty strike at the very heart and display of God's image in humanity of male and female. We must love people, yet discern spirits.

We are not powerless; we are light in the midst of a dark world. Our fasting and intercession with Christ (the great Intercessor) is a powerful weapon for advancing His Kingdom.

191

Remember, earth's battles are first won in the heavenlies, because earth's issues are foremost spiritual ones.

We can't afford to be silent anymore—not in heaven or on earth. We must pray for government leaders, corporate heads, church leaders, and everything that impacts man and land. We know how to communicate with each other, but we must dialogue with the Father, with Jesus, and with Holy Spirit regarding the issues around us. We cannot turn a blind eye. In fact, one of the anointings we carry is that of the open eye!

Let's stand with God regarding our nation and pray for breakthrough with His edicts. He will show us what to do.

THE RISE OF THE FEARLESS

The list is long of women who, through the centuries, dared to move past cultural norms and follow the call of destiny. Women like Aimee Semple-McPherson, Maria Woodworth-Etter, and Kathryn Kuhlman stood amidst mockers and those who cried, "Silence! You're a woman!" But they didn't. And their courage to follow God released heaven's healing over humanity.

Here are just a few other fearless ones among the countless in history:

- Joan of Ark (1417 A.D.) who led an army to national victory at the age of 15.

- Elizabeth Blackwell (1849 A.D.) who pushed past prejudice and became the first woman in the U.S. to receive a medical degree; then, working with two other women, they founded the New York Infirmary for Women and Children that later included a women's college for training doctors, the first of its kind.

- Jane Addams was a pioneer settlement worker, public philosopher, sociologist, author, and leader in women's suffrage and world peace in the early 1900's. In 1931 she became the first American woman to be awarded the Nobel Peace Prize.

- Ida B. Wells was an African-American journalist, editor, and skilled rhetorician who worked for the advancement of African-Americans also in the early 1900's.

- Mother Teresa was founder of the Missionaries of Charity that provides hospices and homes for people with HIV/AIDS, leprosy and tuberculosis, soup kitchens, children's and family counseling programs, orphanages, and schools.

- Rosa Parks simply did the right thing and refused to give up her seat on a bus because of the color of her skin; this fueled the righteous fire for African-American civil rights (1955).

The list is endless of women who have made a difference for their generation, and those to come. However, it doesn't always take grand heroism. It just takes a fearless listening to God and doing what He says, in spite of cultural norms. It takes having a holy backbone as a woman in the home, in the office, and in Church—women who will walk in dignity, delight, and right dominion.

Oh, and by the way, I forgot to add that Joan of Ark was burned at the stake for daring to follow God's voice and make a difference for a nation. She was nineteen at the time.

What is God saying to you? What is your calling? What are your gifts? What is the sphere of influence God has called you to lift into divine destiny? What is the divine weapon God has put in your hand for your territory?

My weapon is my pen and my ink is the Father's love...and I'm writing these words for you that you might know the truth about God and you.

It's time for the *Joan of Arks* to saddle up. It's time for the suitable helper to step into her appointed place.

THE RISE FOR A NATION'S DESTINY

In America, we are a society inundated with messages. In the garden, *Ishshah* only had one dark message to contend with. Today, we are overwhelmed with myriad voices about how to look and what values we should embrace. David Shenk, author of *Data Smog*, shows us that with the advent of technology, the average American is assaulted *daily* by over 6,000 messages, as compared to 560 per day in 1971.[2]

Many of these voices are laced with misogyny (the denigration of women) and misandry (denigration of men). Both play into the war against original design and unity. We saw how misogyny played out in ancient cultures, but today it manifests in other numerous ways, including: discrimination, female denigration, pornography, fashion that exploits girls' body parts, violence against women, and sexual objectification of females. Rape cultures, hip-hop, date-rape, electronic games that glorify, justify, and even normalize the objectification, exploitation, or victimization of women are common place.

These propagate negative stereotyping of women, and the promotion of prostitution and sex-trafficking. In some sub-cultures, derogatory names are often used with hostile representation of the female gender. Many Hip Hop and rap artists use misogynistic lyrics to gain commercial success, but their success is the exploitation of our daughters. Men are "praised if they abuse and exploit women...Insults are used to degrade women and keep them 'in their place'...women are portrayed as good only for sex, are objects of domination for men, and are held as morally and intellectually inferior to men."[3]

Such music is like pouring poison into the brain, altering and programming the mind with destructive beliefs and behavior patterns.

Studies show that in the 1990s, "audiences began to *demand* more violent and offensive lyrics and record executives were urging artists to write them." It was the turn to a culture of violence. This helped to push the door wide open to violence in sexual encounters, including the use of whips, chains, and torture devices as a way to "liven up" sex.

It's not only the boys who adopt these views for a sense of power gone awry, but girls too can internalize these messages against themselves and other females. Original *dominion* has been replaced by the ideology of *domination* as young men are being trained to use their "*Yod*" to oppress rather than serve. And girls are being trained to comply.

Who will teach them their true identity? The fathers and mothers who know the truth will...we must.

We must be aware of these elements that tear at the fabric of a woman's identity and dignity, but also of a man's too, and thus the wellbeing of an entire culture! And we must be more than aware. We must be pro-active to advance love, respect and truth about identity for the healing of lives, and our nation. It is an issue that must be reconciled with heaven's design in our territory.

THE RISE FOR OUR SISTERS

Our life as women is never simply about us. We are meant to help another on their journey into divine destiny. It's easy to live in our routines and not be aware of what's going on around us. Today, many women around the world are still living in a judgment paradigm.

Things such as: abuse, restrictions, gendercide (killing of baby girls in preference of boys), honor killings, sexual servitude, live burials of women with deceased husbands, women told they are born female because of "bad Karma" in their "previous" life and as such, are unable to enter heaven because of their gender, women treated as slaves, and women being made to carry shame simply because they are female, are all still very much a part of this world.

Perhaps you've heard about young Malala Yousafzai, a young Pakistani girl who was shot in the face in October, 2012, by the Taliban. Why? Because she was campaigning for women's rights and girls' education. Her crime was a desire to be educated.[4]

The following are a few other facts of what our sisters are facing. According to *The World's Women 2010: Trends and Statistics,* **reports show that:**[5]

- "Two thirds of the world's adult illiteracy are women." This is critical as "access to education, on all levels, is a focal point in the liberation and promotion of women. Education is the prerequisite for access to employment, to personal autonomy and to complete participation in economic social and political life."

- "Violence against women is a universal phenomenon in which women are subjected to different forms of violence — physical, sexual, psychological and economic - both within and outside their homes."

- "In many regions of the world, longstanding customs put considerable pressure on women to accept being beaten by their husbands, even for trivial reasons. Whether for burning the food, venturing outside without telling their husband, neglecting children or arguing with their husband, in quite a few countries a very high percentage of women themselves consider such behavior sufficient grounds for being physically hit."

- "In certain countries, environmental factors continue to disproportionately affect women as long as gender-differentiated roles and expectations in the household, family and community life are maintained."

- "In some parts of the world… women's lack of access to and control over resources limits their economic autonomy and increases their vulnerability to economic or environmental shocks."

In a WHO (World Health Organization) multi-country study on women's health, reports show the following:[6]

- "The first sexual experience for many women is reported as forced" and that "risk factors for being a victim of sexual violence include ... **attitudes accepting violence and gender inequality**".... Other "factors specifically associated with sexual violence perpetration include: beliefs in family honor and sexual purity, ideologies of male sexual entitlement, and weak legal sanctions for sexual violence."

- Statistics show that violence against women take a huge toll with ripple effects throughout society. "Isolation, inability to work, loss of wages, and limited ability for a woman to care for herself and her children is part of that 'ripple effect.'"

- A shift in cultural discrimination is on the rise in many countries through legislation, **microfinance and gender equality training, and community-based initiatives that address gender inequality, along with communication and relationship skills.**

Violence is not acceptable. Who will stand with these? Who will pray for them and teach them? Who will help them on their journey into a divine destiny?

While a woman's value is at the highest today in many nations, the road of restoration from the Fall continues with many challenges. Oppression against women continues to be "**a global problem of pandemic proportions**," and an important key to this issue is *how women are viewed*. In the U.S. alone, 25% of women will experience abuse as part of a dynamic of control and oppression. My desire is to change this view…beginning with

197

your view of your own identity. It's time to drink from the crystal glass.

Even as I began to write this book, news headlines were ablaze with the story of India's social outrage over a government failure to act with justice regarding rape and the brutal treatment of women. One article called it a "culture crisis" as "*a clash between traditional values and a new generation of educated, modern women whose independence is threatening for some Indian men.*"[7] Even so, many other men are beginning to stand on behalf of women's welfare! Whether they realize it or not, they are hearing God's heartbeat for justice for the daughters.

It's time for truth to overturn fallen traditions. None of us can control what another thinks of us, but we do have the power to choose what we believe and what voice we allow to guide our thoughts. And thoughts, we know, are the spark to action. We must rise and take right action for our sisters, and help them to rise too.

THE RISE OF THE FATHER'S DAUGHTERS

Our Father wants you and I to live vibrantly, dynamically, and empowered as His image on earth. He has removed the hammer that has been held over us, whether by a person, culture, religion, or the dark limitations of our own perceptions. You and I have many gifts to be developed. We must be confident and fearless in letting God direct us into freedom for effective influence in divine purpose.

There are many mountains to climb, changes to ignite, dreams to realize, natural and spiritual children to raise up, and discoveries to pioneer as God's daughters!

It's time for the suitable helpers to arise as fiery *Ezer's* with prophetic vision. It's time for the *daughter of troops* to mount up with the Heavenly Lover of our soul to effect divine good on earth...to return the nations to divine inheritance as we labor together with our brothers in Christ.

You are here for a reason and a purpose. Be confident in your identity in Him. You are not a mistake, an "oops!" or an accident, no matter how you got here. God fashioned you uniquely to live and shine as His image on earth. You have your Father's permission and authority to flourish in every way as you walk arm-in-arm with the Last Adam as His beautiful redeemed *Ishshah*.

I will say this one last time as we close: you are loved, valued, and affirmed by *Elohim*—by Father, Jesus, and Holy Spirit. Your gender is part of His image. It is not a shame. It is a glory. You are a royal daughter for kingly accomplishments. You are not lesser than another, nor made to sit in silence. You are redeemed and you have been given authority. Now, what will you do with it?

Come, let's cross a new threshold together as a company of intuitive helpers who dance with swords in the arms of the Last Adam. We have a work to do for the healing of our homes, communities and nations. It's time to drink from the crystal glass of God's truth, to stand tall and free with arms open wide and our face toward heaven.

Come, let's breathe heaven's atmosphere as we step into our full identity in Christ, clothed in light, as our Father's empowered daughters, for such a time as this.

Our dance opens a portal, our feet shake the ground like drums,
And our hands storm the clouds above, the walls are falling down.
The Glory is here, is invading us, raise up your hands,
And pull down the atmosphere from heaven like a waterfall,
Like a vortex forcing earth into the heavens.
Can you hear the drums?
Do you feel your feet like fire?
Let's storm the heavens together.

- David Munoz
(www.nvtn.org)

ENDNOTES

Chapter 1

1. "Women's History in America," Women's International Center, accessed January 3, 2013, an excerpt from Compton's Interactive Encyclopedia, Copyright (c) 1994, 1995 Compton's NewMedia, Inc., http://www.wic.org/misc/history.htm.
2. Veinot, L.L. (Don), Henzel, Ron, "Bill Gothard's Evangelical Talmud," Midwest Christian Outreach, accessed February 7, 2013. http://www.midwestoutreach.org/mcoijournal/bill-gothards-evangelical-talmud.

Chapter 2

1. Dr. Frank T. Seekins, *Hebrew Word Pictures* (Hebrew World USA, 2012).
2. Ibid.
3. Kevin Conner and Ken Malmin, *The Covenants* (City Bible Publishing, 1997), pp 13.
4. Dr. Frank T. Seekins, *Hebrew Word Pictures* (Hebrew World USA, 2012).
5. "The Letter Yod," Hebrew for Christians, accessed September 6, 2013.
   http://www.hebrew4christians.com/Grammar/Unit_One/Al eph-Bet/Yod/yod.html.
6. Rabbi Aaron L. Raskin, "Shin — The Matriarchs," Chabad.org., accessed September 5th, 2013.

http://www.chabad.org/library/article_cdo/aid/137093/jew ish/Shin-The-Matriarchs.htm.; "Hebrew Numbers," Water in the Dessert, accessed October 1, 2013. http://water-desert.wikifoundry.com/page/Hebrew+Numbers.

7. Noah Webster, "Atonement," *American Dictionary of the English Language, Noah Webster 1828* (New York: Published by S. Converse, 1828).

8. Dr. Frank T. Seekins, *Hebrew Word Pictures* (Hebrew World USA, 2012).

9. "The Letter Hey," Hebrew for Christians, accessed September 1, 2013. http://www.hebrew4christians.com/Grammar/Unit_One/Al eph-Bet/Hey/hey.html.

Chapter 3

1. Dr. Frank T. Seekins, *Hebrew Word Pictures* (Hebrew World USA, 2012).

2. James Hastings, "The Wedding Festivities," *Hastings Dictionary of the Bible* (Hendrickson Publishers 1996), pp 585.

3. Google. "Counterpart," https://www.google.com.

4. F. Brown, S. Driver, and C. Briggs, "Neged," *The Brown-Driver-Briggs Hebrew and English Lexicon* (Hendrickson Publishers, 2008) 617-5057.

Chapter 4

1. Gen. 3:1
2. Gen. 3:3
3. Gen. 3:4-5
4. Gen. 3:6
5. Gen. 3:6
6. Gen. 3:14-15
7. Gen. 3:16
8. Gen. 3:17-19
9. Prov. 2:16; 19:13; 12:4; 21:19; 23:27

Chapter 5

1. Karen Rhea Nemet-Nejat, "Women in Ancient Mesopotamia," *Academia.edu*, accessed August 30, 2013. http://academia.edu/873588/Womens_Roles_in_Ancient_Me sopotamia
2. "The Status of Women in Egyptian Society," *Cornell University Library*, accessed July 7, 2013. http://www.library.cornell.edu/colldev/mideast/womneg.h tm.
3. James, C. Thompson, B.A., M.Ed., *Women in the Ancient World, Introduction*, Revised July, 2010, accessed July 6, 2013. http://www.womenintheancientworld.com/Introduction.ht m.
4. "Women's History in America," Women's International Center, accessed August 8, 2013, an excerpt from Compton's Interactive Encyclopedia Copyright © 1994, 1995 Compton's NewMedia, Inc. http://www.wic.org/misc/history.htm.
5. "The Code of Hammurabi," Wikipedia, accessed August 7, 2013. http://en.wikipedia.org/wiki/Code_of_Hammurabi.
6. Ibid.
7. Ibid.
8. Charles F. Horne, Claude Hermann Walter Johns, "Ancient History Sourcebook: Code of Hammurabi, c. 1780 BCE," Fordham University, accessed January 7, 2013. http://www.fordham.edu/halsall/ancient/hamcode.asp.
9. "The Role of Women," Judaism 101, accessed August 6, 2013. http://www.jewfaq.org/women.html.
10. Ibid.
11. Ibid.
12. Sr. Vincent Emmanuel Hannon, "Women in Ancient Culture," *Catherine College Library*, accessed August 8, 2013. http://www.catherinecollegelibrary.net/classic/hannon2.asp.
13. Dr. Pamela Chrabieh, February 13, 2013, "Women and Religions, Women's Roles and Situations," *Red Lips High Heels*, accessed August 5, 2013.

http://www.redlipshighheels.com/the-veil-in-ancient-middle-easternwestern-asian-cultures/.

14. Sanderson Beck, *Assyrian, Babylonian, and Persian Empires,* accessed August 1, 2013. http://www.san.beck.org/EC6-Assyria.html.

15. Michael D. Marlowe, "Headcovering Customs of the Ancient World," Bible Research, accessed August 10, 2013. http://www.bible-researcher.com/headcoverings3.html.

16. Dr. Pamela Chrabieh, February 13, 2013, "Women and Religions, Women's Roles and Situations," *Red Lips High Heels,* accessed August 5, 2013. http://www.redlipshighheels.com/the-veil-in-ancient-middle-easternwestern-asian-cultures/.

17. Jon Zenz, September 9, 2013, "New Light on Paul and Women," *House2House Magazine,* accessed October 5, 2013. http://house2housemagazine.com/2013/09/09/new-light-on-paul-and-women-by-jon-zens/.

18. Berel Dov Lerner, October 24, 2005, "The Ten Curses of Eve," *Lerner's Jewish Bible Blog,* accessed August 6, 2013. http://jewishbible.blogspot.com/2005/10/ten-curses-of-eve-unpublishable.html.

19. Ibid.

20. Ibid.

21. Ibid.

22. James, C. Thompson, B.A., M.Ed., "Women in Sparta," Women in the Ancient World, Revised July, 2010, accessed August 20, 2013. http://www.womenintheancientworld.com/spartanwomen.htm.

23. "Ancient Greece," Wikipedia, accessed August 20, 2013. http://en.wikipedia.org/wiki/Ancient_Greece.

24. "Greek City States." Crystalinks, accessed August 20, 2013. http://www.crystalinks.com/greekcities.html.

25. James, C. Thompson, B.A., M.Ed., "Women in Ancient Greece," Women in the Ancient World, Revised July, 2010, accessed October 1, 2013. http://www.womenintheancientworld.com/greece.htm

26. "The Women of Athens," *Minnesota State University Mankato,* accessed October 1, 2013. http://www.mnsu.edu/emuseum/prehistory/aegean/cultur e/womenofathens.htm.
27. James, C. Thompson, B.A., M.Ed., "Women in Ancient Greece: What Athenian Men Said About Women," Women in the Ancient World, Revised July, 2010, accessed October 1, 2013. http://www.womenintheancientworld.com/greece.htm.
28. "Women, Gender, and Religion," Creighton University, *Journal of Religion & Society Supplement Series 5,* edited by Susan Calef and Ronald A. Simkins, (The Kripke Center 2009 ISSN: 1941-8450, pp 8-9,), accessed November 5, 2013. http://moses.creighton.edu/jrs/2009/2009-7.pdf.
29. Sr. Vincent Emmanuel Hannon, "Women in Ancient Culture," Catherine College Library, accessed August 8, 2013. http://www.catherinecollegelibrary.net/classic/hannon2.asp.
30. James, C. Thompson, B.A., M.Ed., "Women in Ancient Greece: What Athenian Men Said About Women," Women in the Ancient World, Revised July, 2010, accessed October 1, 2013. http://www.womenintheancientworld.com/greece.htm.
31. "Misogyny," Wikipedia, accessed October 1, 2013. http://en.wikipedia.org/wiki/Misogyny.; Manisha Gupta, "Was Euripedes a Misogynist," *Association of Young Journalists and Writers,* accessed October 2, 2013. http://ayjw.org/print_articles.php?id=15702.; James, C. Thompson, B.A., M.Ed., "Women in Ancient Greece," Women in the Ancient World, Revised July, 2010, accessed October 2, 2013. http://www.womenintheancientworld.com/greece.htm.
32. T. Kester, "Slideshare," posted Nov. 11, 2008, accessed August 1, 2013. www.slideshare.net/tkester/classical-greek-humanism-presentation.

Chapter 6

1. "St. Photini, the Samaritan Woman", Antiochian, Orthodox, Christian Archdiocese, accessed October 31, 2013.

http://www.antiochian.org/node/17560, by permission of the Orthodox Church in America, www.oca.org.

2. See Phil. 4:2-3; 1 Cor. 1:11; Col. 4:15; Acts 1:12-14, 9:36; 16:14; 18:24-26; 21:7-9; 1 Cor. 16:19; Rom. 16:1-16.

Chapter 7

1. Lyn Webster, Wilde, "Did the Amazons Really Exist?," The Women of Action Network, History: Legends, accessed July 8, 2013. http://www.woa.tv/articles/hi_amazonexist.html.; N.S. Gill, "Who Were the Amazons?," About.com, Ancient/Classical History, accessed July 5, 2013. http://ancienthistory.about.com/cs/women1/a/amazons1.ht m.; "Amazons, the Legendary Founders of Ephesus," Ephesus, Mythologies: Amazons, accessed July 6, 2013. http://www.ephesus.us/ephesus/amazons.htm.

2. Tim Challis, June 07, 2011, "Saved Through Childbearing?" Challies, accessed January 1, 2013. http://www.challies.com/articles/saved-through-childbearing.

Chapter 8

1. "State Church of the Roman Empire," Wikipedia, accessed November 12, 2013. http://en.wikipedia.org/wiki/State_church_of_the_Roman_E mpire. "A Brief Biography: Constantine the Great," New Byzantium, accessed November 8, 2013. http://www.new-byzantium.org/Constntne-Bio.html.

2. "Are Women Human Beings," English Translation by John Wijnaards, Catherine of Sienna Virtual College, (original print 1618 A.D., Germany), accessed August 8, 2013. http://www.catherineofsiena.net/about/eugene.asp#script.

3. Ibid.; "Tertullian: Moral Principles," Wikipedia, accessed July 6, 2013. http://en.wikipedia.org/wiki/Tertullian; John Wijnaards, "Women Can be Priests," Women Priests, accessed

August 7, 2013.
http://www.womenpriests.org/traditio/sinful.asp.
4. Ibid.; John Bevere, "Live Extraordinary," *Charisma Magazine*, Martin Luther works quoted, accessed October 1, 2013. http://www.charismamag.com/spirit/devotionals/live-extraordinarily?view=article&id=16544:discover-your-authority-in-christ&catid=1543.
5. "Tertullian," Wikipedia, accessed June 1, 2013. http://en.wikipedia.org/wiki/Tertullian.
6. "On the Apparel of Women," New Advent, Translated by S. Thelwall. From Ante-Nicene Fathers, Vol. 4. Edited by Alexander Roberts, James Donaldson, and A. Cleveland Coxe. (Buffalo, NY: Christian Literature Publishing Co., 1885.) Revised and edited for New Advent by Kevin Knight. http://www.newadvent.org/fathers/0402.htm.; John Wijnaards, "Women Can be Priests," Women Priests, accessed August 7, 2013. http://www.womenpriests.org/traditio/sinful.asp.
7. Valerie Tarico, "20 Vile Quotes Against Women By Religious Leaders From St. Augustine to Pat Robertson," AlterNet, accessed August 9, 2013. http://www.alternet.org/belief/20-vile-quotes-against-women-religious-leaders-st-augustine-pat-robertson.
8. Ibid.
9. John Wijnaards, "Women Can be Priests," Women Priests, accessed August 7, 2013. http://www.womenpriests.org/traditio/tertul.asp.; "Are Women Human Beings," English Translation by John Wijnaards, , Catherine of Sienna virtual College, (original print 1618 A.D., Germany), accessed August 8, 2013. http://www.catherineofsiena.net/about/eugene.asp#script.
10. Henry Morehouse Taber, *Faith or Fact* (New York, Peter Eckler, Publisher, 1897), pp.11.
11. Marie, I George, "What Aquinas Really Said About Women," First Things, Issue Archive 1999, accessed August 11, 2013. http://www.firstthings.com/article/2007/01/what-aquinas-really-said-about-women-24; "Statements on Women by

Church Fathers, Doctors, and Saints," Spring Hill College, online Library, accessed on Aug. 12, 2013. http://www.shc.edu/theolibrary/resources/women.htm.

12. Ibid.

13. John Bevere, "Live Extraordinary," Charisma Magazine, accessed October 1, 2013. http://www.charismamag.com/spirit/devotionals/live-extraordinarily?view=article&id=16544:discover-your-authority-in-christ&catid=1543; Rowland Croucher, "Martin Luther," John Mark Ministries, accessed August 3, 2013. http://www.jmm.org.au/articles/14223.htm.

14. "Theophraste Renaudot (1586-1653), General Collection of Discourses of the Virtuosi of France," Volume 2: Conference 105, pp 31-37; 35-37, University of Florida, accessed August 3, 2013. http://web.clas.ufl.edu/users/ufhatch/pages/02-TeachingResources/ClioElectric/1-Electronic%20Texts/Renaudot%20Conferences/10-Renaudot-Conference%202-035-Women%20&%20Learning.pdf.

15. "The Gospel of Thomas," Wikipedia, accessed August 4, 2013. http://en.wikipedia.org/wiki/Gospel_of_Thomas.

16. Tim Keller, "The Gnostics and Jesus," Redeemer Perspectives, March 2004, accessed August 6, 2013. http://reformedperspectives.org/articles/tim_keller/tim_kell er.GnosticsandJesus.html.

17. Philip Pullella, July 29, 2013, "Pope says gays must not be judged or marginalized," Reuters, accessed July 29, 2013. http://www.reuters.com/article/2013/07/29/us-pope-gays-idUSBRE96S0DX20130729.

Chapter 9

1. Richard S. Cervin, "Does 'Kephale' Mean 'Source' or 'Authority Over' in Greek Literature?: A Rebuttal," CBE International, accessed on July 29, 2013. http://www.cbeinternational.org/?q=content/does-kephale-mean-source-or-authority-over-greek-literature-rebuttal.

2. Ibid.

3. "Domestic Violence: Statistics and Facts," Safe Horizon, accessed August 4, 2013. http://www.safehorizon.org/index/what-we-do-2/domestic-violence--abuse-53/domestic-violence-the-facts-195.html.
4. Chuck Colson, October 20, 2009, "Domestic Violence Within the Church: The Ugly Truth," Religion Today, accessed August 9, 2013. http://www.religiontoday.com/news/domestic-violence-within-the-church-the-ugly-truth-11602500.html; Barrington H. Brennen, "Why Do Christian Husbands Abuse Their Wives? Part One," Sounds of Encouragement, accessed November 2, 2013. http://www.soencouragement.org/whyabuse.htm; "Domestic Violence," The Clark County Prosecuting Attorney, accessed November 7, 2013. http://www.clarkprosecutor.org/html/domviol/facts.htm; "Domestic Violence" Olivette, Missouri, Departments and Services, Police, Stop Violence Against Women, cited Oct. 6, 2013. http://www.olivettemo.com/pView.aspx?id=2419&catid=29.

Chapter 10

1. Andrea Roltgen, "Feminism: The Caustic Explosion That is Destroying America," Freedom Outpost, posted Feb. 21, 2013, accessed July 7, 2013. http://freedomoutpost.com/2013/02/feminism-the-caustic-explosion-that-is-destroying-america/#ixzz2LaLFUuss.
2. "Gender Roles in Christianity," Wikipedia, accessed August 9, 2013. http://en.wikipedia.org/wiki/Gender_roles_in_Christianity.

Chapter 11

1. Gus, Lubin, December 30, 2013, "How Stalin Defeated Christmas and Forever Changed the Day when Russians Get

Presents," SF Gate, accessed January 1, 2014.
http://www.sfgate.com/technology/businessinsider/article/
How-Stalin-Defeated-Christmas-And-Forever-Changed-
5102351.php.

2. David Shenk, *Data Smog: Surviving the Information Glut*, Harper
   Edge, 1997 ISBN 0-06-018701-8.
3. "Misogyny in Hip Hop Culture," Wikipedia, accessed June 30,
   2013.
   http://en.wikipedia.org/wiki/Misogyny_in_hip_hop_culture
   .
4. James Meikle, February 4, 2013, "Malala Yousafzai: God has
   given me a second life," The Guardian, accessed June 3, 2013.
   http://www.guardian.co.uk/world/2013/feb/04/malala-
   yousafzai-god-second-life.
5. "The World's Women 2010: Trends and Statistics," United
   Nations Statistics Division, accessed February 20, 2013.
   http://unstats.un.org/unsd/demographic/products/Worlds
   women/Executive%20summary.htm.
6. "Violence Against Women," World Health Organization,
   Updated October 2013, accessed November 5, 2013.
   http://www.who.int/mediacentre/factsheets/fs239/en/.
7. Holly Williams, February 19, 2013, "Brutal gang-rape sparks
   culture crisis in India," CBS News, accessed, February 20,
   2013. http://www.cbsnews.com/8301-18563_162-
   57570164/brutal-gang-rape-sparks-culture-crisis-in-india/.

MORE BOOKS BY
J. NICOLE WILLIAMSON

The Esther Mandate
The War for America's Destiny

Heaven's Secret
of Success
*Cultivating Your Identity
from Seed to Harvest*

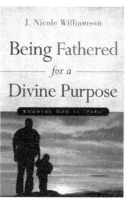

Being Fathered
for a Divine Purpose
*Knowing God
as "Papa"*

These books can be purchased at:
www.kingslantern.com
www.amazon.com